BICYCLING THE MIDWEST

DIANA MILESKO-PYTEL

Contemporary Books, Inc.
Chicago

Library of Congress Cataloging in Publication Data

Milesko-Pytel, Diana.
    Bicycling the Midwest.

    Includes index.
        1. Cycling—Middle West—Guide-books.   2. Camp sites,
facilities, etc.—Middle West—Guide-books.   3. Middle
West—Description and travel—Guide-books.   I. Title.
GV1045.5.M55M54   1979   917.7   78-73672
ISBN 0-8092-7608-9
ISBN 0-8092-7607-0 pbk.

Published by Contemporary Books, Inc.
180 North Michigan Avenue, Chicago, Illinois 60601
Manufactured in the United States of America
Library of Congress Catalog Card Number: 78-73672
International Standard Book Number: 0-8092-7608-9 (cloth)
                                                    0-8092-7607-0 (paper)

Published simultaneously in Canada by
Beaverbooks
953 Dillingham Road
Pickering, Ontario L1W 1Z7
Canada

To S. J., who leads by following.

Contents

Utensils; Shelter; Clothing; Luxuries and Other Personal
Items; First Aid.

Green Trail and Map; Baraboo and the Wisconsin Dells
Trail and Map; Mississippi River from LaCrosse to
Cassville Trail and Map; Door County from Sturgeon Bay
to Gills Rock Trail and Map; Hayward to Bayfield and
the Apostle Islands Trail and Map.

Acknowledgments

Many good friends, fellow bikers, and authorities on various subjects gave their time and expertise to help get this book rolling. I would particularly like to thank the following people who shared their experiences and knowledge, and gave me support: Joseph E. Bares, Debra Singer, Don Algrim, Toni Milesko, Phyllis Harmon, Jim Kehew, Fritzi Soutsos, Ron Boi, Dave Callsen, Gene and Ann Weisbecker, Dewey Chiesel, Marcie Telander, Tom Knecht, Fred Cornforth, Ed Blackman, Helen Hayes, Judy Kolstad, and Jim and Hedy Moore. Members of the League of American Wheelmen have been more than helpful in gathering information on bicycling trails in the Midwest.

I am especially grateful for the patience, understanding and enduring support of Frank, Deidre, Melissa, and Roman Pytel.

1

The Civilized Sport

The whole world is empty except for the three bikers gliding downhill ahead of you. Morning fog, locked in low pockets in the cornfields, contrasts with the sweet and brilliant sunlight that is sharp and warm on your face. You lean over your handlebars, wind in your teeth. As you bank into a turn, you tuck your body into a tight ball. Following the dots on the highway fills you with a strange and foolish joy; you're nothing but a pair of eyes watching an early autumn country-side float past. How clever of nature, matching the rusts, greens, reds and oranges with the waterfalls, islands and bluffs. This is the biking you came for.

You soar through the dip at the bottom of the hill and your momentum carries you halfway up the next rise. You're cruising at about 30 miles an hour when a station wagon pulls up, riding parallel to you. Reluctantly, you brake, to let it pass. Your momentum is gone, and now comes the work. Your body rocks first to one side of the bike and then the other as you put all the muscle you've got, which amounts to several hundred pounds per square inch, onto the rattrap pedals. You move back into the climbing position, and the sun, reflecting from inside your front wheel rim, sparkles in your head.

The hill flattens out just enough for you to establish a new pace, and the tension on your crank eases. You flip into first gear and, with your friends at the top cheering you, press on to the crest of the hill. This is the challenge you came for.

Biking is an ideal exercise, resulting in physical fitness, self-discovery, and a greater understanding of the world. It gives the robustness and vigor of a regular workout and satisfies the inherent desire in all of us to go someplace different. Millions of Americans find the harmony between human muscle and man's greatest invention, the wheel, is a perfect antidote to the fatigue caused by today's hectic living. Biking is one of the safest sports around, if done with common sense. It is an interesting, social, educational, and civilized activity that benefits your heart, lungs, back muscles, arm muscles, leg muscles, and varicose veins.

Regular cycling can be a family activity which is healthy, social, and educational. Whether you travel with family or friends, you will certainly know your fellow riders better after a bike trip.

WHY BIKE IN THE MIDWEST?

You may have heard that traveling through the Midwest is monotonous. By car, perhaps. But on a bike, everything is closer, more intimate, and more physical. Linger over the sight of a country lake casting off the early morning sun's rays, be tickled by the tree-shaded dips and curves of a road following a moraine, or wonder at the sultry, secret marshes that cushion the vast Mississippi. The Midwest offers a wealth of scenery, from farmland and pasture, to waterfalls, islands, bluffs, and ravines. It is the ideal place for a civilized cyclist to increase his touring experience while thoroughly enjoying himself.

There are no burning deserts, exhausting mountains or oceans to cross in this part of the country. Unlike some

Two-wheeled tranquility—a great escape from the pressures of modern life.

Eastern and Western mountain roads, there are no 15 percent grades that everyone except the toughest athlete has to walk his bike up. But the Midwest has hundreds of areas with rollercoaster hills—half of which are down—that delight the two-wheeled traveler.

The long and lovely biking season runs from early spring through late fall in most Midwestern states. Hearty cyclists even bike in winter, when the weather is dry, taking "icicle bicycle" or "frozen dozen" trips of 10 to 15 miles with friends. If you are properly and warmly dressed, cycling in winter can be less hazardous than biking on a humid summer day.

WHAT BIKING DOES FOR YOU

There used to be a saying that whenever an American got the feeling he ought to get some exercise, he would lie down until the feeling went away. Not so today. Exercise has

This sunbather's solitude would be impossible without a bike.

become a movement in this country, nurtured by a new type of activist who cares about diet, muscle tone, and physical endurance.

Such concern is good, but the best kind of exercise is that which is done first because it is fun, and then because it is good for you. If exercise is painful or results in injury, it's not fulfilling its purpose, namely, to get you to feel better about yourself and your surroundings and to make you healthier.

People of any age and almost any physical condition can enjoy this sport, for it stimulates both the mind and body, and can be done as strenuously as you choose. After a cycling jaunt you can say, "What a good trip! I had a good time!" and you are being honest. You may have fond memories of cycling with your friends toward the Chicago skyline, which rests on the horizon like a noble mountain range. After riding through foothills of suburbs with their low, single family homes, you thread your way through yawning city canyons and finally arrive at your destination, a smiling Lake Michigan decorated with lacy white caps.

Unlike team sports, biking doesn't depend upon raising enough players to get a game going. Nor do you worry about thwacking a ball, winning, or doing more sit-ups than you did yesterday. Your eyes, ears, nose, and intellect can absorb the world around you. If you are tired at the end of the day, it is a relaxed tiredness. The rhythm of pedaling paces the beat of your heart and lungs, putting you in tune with your body and your surroundings.

I earned my first bike by selling newspaper subscriptions at the age of 10, and wouldn't let anyone else ride it. No wonder, for it gave me freedom. I got lost and then found myself, tracing zig-zag paths through the gridiron street pattern of Chicago's South Side. I prayed for sunny weather, not to keep dry as much as to use the sun to tell directions.

I pedaled down Halsted Street to the Stockyards, smelling the pungent odor of slaughtered animals, and watched, fascinated, as big cattle trucks pulled in and out of the stockyards' arched gates.

Working my way south to Beverly Hills, I saw big houses I thought only existed in "Father Knows Best," with shiny red wagons, rollerskates, and other toys left carelessly on manicured lawns, where someone could steal them—but no one did.

Often I biked with a best friend, whomever that happened to be at the moment; just as often I went alone, delighting in the adventure, and enduring the inconveniences, such as a sudden rainstorm, a parched throat, or a strong headwind. When I miscalculated my energy and biked farther than I should have, I learned that the swimmer's precaution, "Turn around before you use half your energy, for you still must get back to shore," also applied to cycling.

Biking gives you freedom, opens you to new experiences, and increases your faith in people.

If you pull into a gas station in a car, the most civility you're likely to get is to have someone wash your windows, unless the pump is self-service. Pull into a gas station on bikes, however, and immediately people come up and ask where you're going, how much gear you're carrying, where you're from. This interest is genuine and they'll happily sit and chat for as long as you want. When you bike, most people see you as a sturdy, yet vulnerable, individual. You become a living example of the pioneering spirit and rugged individualism that molded our nation.

Biking is a means of celebrating the great simplicities in life, such as sunny mornings, happy surprises, children, good humor, and kind deeds. This is a sport for friendly and trusting people who recognize beauty.

IT IS UNCOMPLICATED

Learning to ride a bike is as easy as falling off a horse, but you don't have as far to fall. Most people can learn to ride in half-a-dozen tries. And have you ever met a person who used to know how to bike, but forgot? Like walking, balancing on two wheels becomes almost reflex, once you learn.

Overhauling a cycle is also fairly simple. Unlike a car, all the moving parts on a bike are either exposed, or easily accessible. Once you find out what they do, you can adjust, clean and reassemble most of them yourself. Keep track of how you take it apart and use a *gentle* touch. Ham-fisted pounding on cotter pins and other small parts causes big damage to your crank, headset, and freewheel.

The first several times you work on it, have a friend who knows how to overhaul a bike watch you. If you have an old, coaster-brake type lying around unused in the back of your garage, pull it out, take it apart, and see how it works. The best way to learn how to assemble a bike is by doing it. If the worst happens, and after you put it back together, you find yourself with a dozen leftover nuts and washers, simply sweep them into a brown bag, take the whole mess down to your local cycle shop, and have them reassemble it for you.

DON'T, however, practice fixing your bike right before you take it out on a trip. Get it in tip-top mechanical shape several days before you leave so that you can find any bugs and take care of them. Few things are more frustrating than mechanical trouble on the road.

Other than an occasional overhauling (how often depends upon where, and how often, you ride), caring for a bike is simple. Keep it dry, lubricated, and tightened up. There are many good bike maintenance books on the market to show you how. *Glenn's Complete Bicycle Manual,* by Clarence W. Coles and Harold T. Glenn (Crown Publishers, New York), is useful because it has step-by-step photos of how to take your bike apart and reassemble it, and gives exploded-view diagrams of just about every internal moving part.

IT IS FUNCTIONAL

Biking is fun, but it is also excellent transportation—to a friend's house, to work, and to the supermarket (as long as you remember you're on a bike, and don't buy five bags of groceries). The more you bike the further you'll want to go. The further you go, the better shape you'll be in to go even further. Soon you'll want to take weekend trips into the country, or long journeys through several states.

IT IS INEXPENSIVE

Biking cost three cents a mile in 1977, according to a civil servant who asked the government to reimburse him about $50 for the mileage he pedaled on official errands. He rode 1,635 miles on state business. Had he used his car, the government would have owed him about $250, based on a rate of 15 cents a mile. Had he used his car, the government would have paid the $250 without question. But because he biked, saved money, cut down on pollution, and got exercise while running state errands, it took a two-year brouhaha before he got his check.

Biking is so cheap, people won't believe it. After bike-camping for two weeks in the Appalachian Mountains in 1977, three friends and I split the bill. The total included several hearty meals at fine Southern restaurants, one motel stay, gas for the car that transported us and our bikes from Chicago to Tennessee, and bus fare for two from Roanoke, Va., back to Knoxville, Tenn., to get the car at the end of the trip. We each paid less than $70.

The American Youth Hostels estimated that the average biker who stayed at hostels spent about $4 a day cycling in 1975. Considering inflation, this is approximately what we spent, for we camped instead of hosteled.

GETTING IN SHAPE

Most adults have many responsibilities and can't spend a lot of time getting in shape for a bike trip. Most younger people have firm, pliable bodies and don't need a lot of time getting in shape. There are many methods of getting in shape. This is the one I use. Tone your muscles for the weekend or week-long trip by biking an hour each day, jumping rope and doing isometric exercises.

To prepare for a week or longer bike trip, take several 50-mile day trips, and a few weekend trips. To get ready for these shorter trips, make biking for an hour each day part of your routine. Start with a pace that you feel is perhaps too easy, and go up gradually from that. You won't get too stiff, suffer pulled muscles or hurt yourself if you take it slow at first. Biking each day should be an activity you look forward to. By the end of several weeks, your stamina will have increased considerably, and you may be getting between 8 and 15 miles per hour regularly, a respectable pace for a civilized biker.

Find a quiet road or bike path for your workouts, one that has little traffic and no lights to slow you down. If you have physical problems that worry you, consult your doctor before beginning your routine.

Pack all your travel gear on the cycle once or twice to give you practice in loading the bike evenly, to get the feel of a fully packed bike, and to let you know what needs repair or adjustment.

Jump rope several minutes a day. Here, too, gradually

These college kids know that bikes are a cheap and convenient way to get around.

increase the number of times you jump according to what is comfortable. As your muscle tone and wind increase, it will be easier to jump longer. This exercise is good for the heart, lungs, arms, and legs. Alternate jumping with your right foot forward for several minutes, then your left foot, and finally with both feet jumping together. Do an equal number of jumps all three ways.

Isometric exercises simply consist of tensing your muscles for several seconds at a time. Do this with the muscles of your thighs, calves, arms and stomach while you sit at work, ride the train, or walk.

PLANNING YOUR TRIP

Half the fun of taking a trip is in the planning, my dad used to say. Then he'd bury himself in maps, encyclopedias, budget

books, and lists of things to take. He had to figure out how to
stuff nine people and their belongings into our 1950 Nash, and
how to get the most interesting vacation for his money.

The same is true for biking. Planning who to go with,
where to go, how to get there, and what to take are
important considerations. Figuring them out is fun.

Your bike route should be mapped out in detail before you
ever swing your leg over the saddle. Don't expect to get
helpful answers if you get lost while biking, for you use
country and other secondary roads. Most people tell you how
to get someplace on big highways if you ask for directions, so
their advice won't be very helpful. Get a good map, mark
your route clearly on it, and then be alert for the landmarks
that tell you where to turn.

Be careful when packing; anything you take "just in case"
will travel with you the whole trip. Don't be like one biker
who set out for a month-long trip through Michigan and
Canada. After two days he sent a box home with 10 pounds of
things he decided he'd really rather pedal without. If you need
an extra sweatshirt or change of socks, buying them at a local
shop gives you a souvenir from your trip.

Don't make such a tight schedule that you can't keep it.
Allow enough time to see the more interesting parts of the
country you ride through. A civilized biker is not concerned
with accruing miles but in learning more about the land and
the people he visits. If you give yourself an extra day or two
you won't have to bypass an attraction with the regret, "Gee,
I wish I had time to see that." You may never go that way
again.

Family bike trips to areas of historical interest, such as New
Salem Park in Illinois, are marvelous ways to teach children
about the history of our country. Adults learn something, too.

HOW TO GET THERE

Trains, buses, and airplanes now accept bikes as a single piece
of luggage. Sometimes there is an extra charge for carrying
your bike; other times you must crate it. If you plan to get to

your biking area on public transportation, call ahead to see what charges and other requirements the company has.

The most common, and easiest, way to get to a "take-off" point, is to drive with the bikes atop your car, on a bike carrier. If you'll be gone for several days, find someplace to park your car that's safe, legal, and inexpensive. Some rangers at national parks will let you park your car in a visitors' center parking lot for a week or so.

WHOM TO INVITE

Most of the time, biking is a social activity. If you travel with others, everyone in the party should be in approximately the same physical condition so that you keep together, share the joys of the trip, and give each other a hand if the need arises. If you bike with your family, or with individuals whose abilities are considerably different, accept the fact that you can go only as far as your weakest member. If a strong rider, such as a teenager, wants to forge ahead of the rest, be sure everyone knows where the other members of the party will be, and have a meeting place up the road. If the slower riders don't catch up within a given time the strong biker should turn back to look for them on the route.

Your last rider should be the most experienced one so he or she can help with flat tires, sickness, etc. He or she should also carry the first aid and patch kits.

It's nice if everyone has the same type of bike, preferably a 10-speed lightweight bike. If some of the group members use balloon tires and others have 10-speeds (common when families ride together), realize that those riding the fat tires must work much harder to go the same distance.

Yet such a mix of bikes can work. Our family biked the Sparta-Elroy trail in Wisconsin a few years ago when the children rode banana-seat, fat-tire bikes. The adults had 10-speeds. We stopped often, enjoyed the scenery, and kept together, not caring how far we were able to go. By the end of the day, we had traveled a very pleasant 45 miles, fat tires and all.

When you choose companions for a bike trip, invite people who enjoy being outdoors, who don't discourage easily, who are easy-going, and, most importantly, who have a sense of humor. A sense of the ridiculous is a sterling quality in a companion when your sunny day is quenched by a series of chilling thunderstorms, or your top-of-the-line bike gets three flats in an afternoon.

HOW MANY PEOPLE

Unless you bike with an organization such as the League of American Wheelmen, who make efficient and complex preparations for a trip, keep your group small. Invite two or three friends at most, or no more than two families. The more people you have on a weekend or longer tour, the more elaborate preparations you need, the more problems you'll have getting everyone to do the same thing at the same time, and the greater difficulty you'll have getting reservations at lodges, restaurants, and camping areas. About the only thing that doesn't increase with the number of bikers is the chance of rain.

This is not true for bike trips that last only one day, however. Invite a dozen or more people on a one-day trip if you want to, for it lasts only four to six hours and is over by 4 p.m. Be sure that everyone in your party has all the important information, and have your group use the buddy system. If you get lost, it's much nicer to get lost in twos.

So that no one does get lost, duplicate all important information and hand it out to everyone. Include a map of the route, meeting places, special landmarks you'll stop to see, lunch stops, and the ending place and approximate quitting time. Even here, break up into smaller groups, for some riders like to travel faster than others. One person should be responsible to see that everyone makes it to the finishing point.

HOW FAR

There are individuals who bike 200 miles a day, but more

than likely you aren't one of them, nor do you want to be. A long run can be a challenge, but most civilized bikers prefer to sightsee on their trip. Rather than listen to the odometer click away the miles, they'll stop and listen to a wedge of mallard ducks honking their way south, or watch a thousand gulls from Lake Michigan peck for insects in a newly turned Wisconsin hayfield. Twenty to fifty miles a day on fairly level ground, with little headwind, is a pleasant pace, and allows for stops at points of interest.

HAVE A DESTINATION

Ask three friends to bike all day with you and chances are good that they'll find other plans, even if it's to watch reruns on TV. Ask them if they want to bike 50 miles to the state border and there may be arguments, but you'll end up biking together, even if it's to a different target than you first suggested.

Biking is more fun when you have a destination. As a child, I rode with vague goals in mind—to see what was south of 63rd Street, to find out how big Marquette Park was, to see where Kedzie Avenue ended.

Specific goals give purpose to adult bike trips also. Historical landmarks, archeological sites, museums, and unspoiled terrain such as marshes, hills, and lakes are good biking targets.

Small goals within your ride are also important. Before you begin a day trip, decide where to have lunch, then be certain there's someplace to purchase a meal when you stop, or pack your lunch. Finding that the only restaurant in town is closed because of fire is merely annoying when you travel by car. On a bike, such a discovery is debilitating, for food is your fuel. Not to have it when you need it taxes the body and the patience beyond civility.

The same holds true for water. Always carry a pint bottle on your frame and don't be shy about getting it refilled at gas stations, drinking fountains, wells, and even private homes and farmhouses, if you are tactful and polite. One hot summer day we flagged down a recreational vehicle on a country road when we couldn't find water anywhere else. Biking brings out the generous side of most people, who are generally happy to share your adventure in some small way, even if it's just to give you water. They may think you're crazy, but they admire your guts.

When your bottle is full, make maximum use of the supply by drinking a few ounces from it several times an hour.

HOW LONG

Plan to bike up to six hours a day (less if you want to do a lot of sightseeing), and figure on quitting about 4 p.m. You may find yourself on the road later than that because of foul weather, a strong headwind, terrain that is hillier than you anticipated, or an especially interesting landmark. By planning to quit at 4 p.m., you should be off the road by dusk at the latest.

In all of your planning, keep in mind that biking is the ideal pastime for a civilized cyclist who believes that exercise, like everything else in life, should be as pleasant as possible, and at the same time serve a useful purpose.

THREE TYPES OF TRIPS

Biking falls into three basic categories, but there are variations and modifications for each of them.

Day trips last one day, are from two to six hours long, and end at 4 p.m. Start from home or carry your bikes via car to a designated area. Choose an interesting destination, such as a museum or park, for lunch; look around, and then head back.

Packing for these trips is simple. Include lunch, water bottle, a few tools and patch kit, air pump, windbreaker, suntan lotion, and, if rain is possible, a poncho. Sometimes day bikers ride to a restaurant and back. This is a good way to eat heartily without feeling overstuffed for long. However, relax for an hour and give your food a chance to digest before you return home.

Use any model bike on a day trip as long as you can keep

Bike tourists like to find colorful, out-of-the-way places to eat—like this spot on Wisconsin's Sugar River Trail.

up with your group on it. Ten-speed bikes are the most comfortable for all trips.

Bike tours are similar to day trips in that you travel light. Bike for a weekend or more but stay in motels and eat in restaurants, eliminating your need for tents, sleeping gear, and cooking equipment. These tours last several days, or weeks, or as long as your money holds out. This type of trip appeals to an employed person who knows the ultimate worth of a soft bed, warm shower, and three, or preferably five, very square meals a day.

Large bike tours sponsored by an organization have sag wagons. These vehicles follow the biking pack and pick up cyclists who have mechanical difficulties so that no one is stranded on the road, homeless and hungry, when evening comes.

In all of your biking, get off the road by dusk. No matter how many lights, orange flags, white shirts or yellow reflectors you have, and no matter which way they wave, bounce, or tumble, motorists won't see you. Car drivers look for other cars, not bikes. Worst of all, a biker can't see dangers until he is on them. Potholes, glass, and other junk on the road could cause a serious mishap.

Travel light when bike touring, but take more than just your charge card. Rain gear, personal items, water bottles (two, if you sweat a lot), a change of clothing, tools, patch kit and air pump, and emergency food such as "gorp," raisins, or other fruit are the minimum.

It is crucial that tourers make all reservations for lodging well in advance and then call to confirm them. Since you have to stick close to your planned itinerary, give yourself plenty of time for unexpected delays.

Bike camping trips are the most freeing, most exciting, and most satisfying method of cycling. They are also the most work, from the planning period to the final pedal stroke.

In bike camping you are totally independent of outside help, for you carry your food, cooking utensils, tools, sleeping gear, and shelter (tent) on your bike. It's nice to have two or three companions on this type of trip, not only to share the fun, but to help carry the load. You need only one set of tools and cooking utensils, whether you have one, or four, bikers. Splitting up the gear makes it lighter for everyone. Each person still carries his or her own clothing, personal items, and luxuries, such as cameras.

Bike camping can be a weekend affair, or it can last several weeks or longer. On a recent trip we met an individual who had been on the road for five months, had biked 9,000 miles alone on his 10-speed, and had traveled the perimeter of the United States. He was finally heading back home to Michigan, only 1,000 miles to go!

Forty pounds is the maximum load an individual can handle comfortably on a 10-speed bike. It will be a challenge to get everything you need into your pannier bags. If you carry more than 40 pounds it will be impossible to remain civilized, so do without the aftershave, perfume, and other luxuries.

Do invest in a good set of pannier bags. Loading gear

Load your
panniers carefully—
so the weight is
evenly distributed.

precariously atop a back wheel in garbage bags or carrying it in a backpack have been done, but both methods raise your center of gravity, drastically increase your fatigue, make biking hazardous, and diminish your fun. Pannier bags fit across the front or rear wheel, and make biking safe, comfortable and efficient. As they are compartmentalized, you can find your toothbrush without unpacking all the cooking and camping gear.

Some people use a handlebar bag for oft-needed items such as camera, sunglasses, and wallets. Many handlebar bags also have a plastic viewing pouch where you can slide in a map and have it in front of you for quick reference. Handlebar bags give extra protection for fragile items such as glasses, and help distribute the weight. Just be sure you don't overload your bike because you have an extra pouch to carry things in.

If you don't use a handlebar bag you can carry your wallet and glasses in a belt pouch which slips onto your belt. If you put your camera in your rear wheel pannier, be sure not to drop your bike.

In bike camping you can make last-minute changes of plans, stay longer at an area you like, or "slightsee" (take a quick look) at one that doesn't seem as interesting as you thought it would be. Since everything you need is on your back wheel, you needn't worry about food or lodging, except to find someplace to pitch your tent. Campgrounds are best for this, as they offer security, stores, washrooms, water, and sometimes showers and laundromats. But in a pinch, graveyards, forests, and prairies can do. Generally speaking, the further you are away from civilization, the freer you are to camp where you please. We couldn't make our planned campground before dark one night, so we asked for permission, then staked out tents in a village churchyard.

When you bike camp, figure out where you can purchase food a day in advance, and buy three meals worth of supplies at about 4 p.m., just before you stop for the day. Make supper your big meal; you'll eat much of the bulk and won't have to carry it; you'll have all night to digest the food, and a hearty meal before retiring helps you to sleep warmer.

Bike camping is much less expensive than touring, and you are closer to nature, and can study her moods. On one trip, when the children still rode in bike seats, it rained during the night. The next morning, four-year-old Melissa climbed out of the tent and observed, "It sure is hazel out." Three-year-old Roman, her sidekick, crawled out and disagreed. "It's not hazel, it's froggy," in his own little boy croak. Both of them enjoyed the early morning mist that washed their cheeks and lashes, fine as seltzer spray.

OTHER WAYS OF BIKING

There are variations to these three methods of biking. One is to mix camping with staying at lodges, or to alternate cooking your own meals with eating in restaurants. This plan offers a change of pace, especially if you're on the road a week or longer. Hot showers, clean sheets, and a laundromat offer a physical and spiritual rebirth after several days on the saddle and nights in a tent.

Another combination is staying in youth hostels and camping. For a nominal membership fee you can join the American Youth Hostels, regardless of your age. Members can stay in hostels—simple overnight accommodations in scenic, historic, and cultural areas—for a small charge. For information and a membership application write:

> National Office
> American Youth Hostels
> Delaplane, Virginia 22025

Whichever method you choose, you'll find biking a peaceful pastime for healthy persons of all ages. Watching the country-side pass through its seasons, just as it has for thousands of years, makes a biker timeless.

WHAT YOU LEARN

You learn about yourself. You find that in certain respects, your body operates much like a machine; it must be cared for properly, or it won't work efficiently. You learn to recognize your limitations and strengths, and find that the physical and emotional needs of others may differ considerably from your own. You learn to give biking all you've got, and then to give yourself credit for the job you do.

WHAT THIS BOOK IS GOOD FOR

Any experienced cyclist can plan a bike trip by looking at a map, deciding on a place that interests him, find county and other secondary roads that link together and are paved, and then pedal off. If your party is small, such trips are infinitely flexible. If you come to a fork in the road and suddenly see that your planned route parallels a cement factory, but the other path is tree-canopied, and winds through hills and farmland, you won't hesitate to change your plans.

If, however, the other road frames a municipal garbage dump instead of a pastoral delight, your ride can be disappointing, if not sickening.

This book was written to help you avoid such disappointments. It is a guide to bike tours in the Midwest which are scenic, varied, and interesting to the intermediate biker. An intermediate biker is one who can average between 20 and 60 miles a day on a trip that may have some hills and auto traffic. This mileage is flexible, however. You may travel considerably less on days when a renovated saw mill, a museum, a restored pioneer town, or simply a tempting lake for swimming, is on your agenda.

On the other hand, you can make moderate biking challenging by increasing the distance you go each day. Seasoned cyclists ride century trips (100 miles) without trouble in a day. Most of the time, however, it is more enjoyable not to hurry, taking in the view as it rolls easily past.

Biking trails in Illinois, Indiana, Iowa, Michigan, Minnesota, and Wisconsin are listed. Several trails in each state are given. Day trips, bike tours, or bike camping are possible on many of them.

This is a guide for the civilized biker and his friends or family, for anyone who is interested in learning about the world and thereby about himself, rather than for the long-distance, endurance rider. Trails are of moderate length, from 50 to 300 miles, and information on destinations is given.

Historical sights, landmarks and festivals are included, as is information on camping, lodging and restaurants. Information on terrain is general (level, hilly, steep) and comes, for the most part, from individuals who have biked the area. Distance given in miles, is necessarily approximate, as all maps and odometers are not completely accurate.

The routes range from flat to hilly, but none are too hard for a biker who uses common sense. Remember, there is nothing wrong with walking your bike up a hill that is too steep to pedal. Almost every biker has done it at one time or another. The number of days given for each trip is the time it will take for leisurely biking. It doesn't include a day of sightseeing. Young, hearty cyclists can cut some of the times in half.

The trips were chosen partly because they make good biking, and partly to get you into a particular area of the state. Once there, hopefully you will find other places nearby to bike through. The trips listed are suggested tours; you can lengthen or shorten them according to your preference.

Chapter 11 is devoted to creating your own route. Gathering together material for a well-planned bike route takes time, but it can be fun.

Rather than repeat trips listed in other sources, I have tried to find previously unpublished routes for the most part.

Included in the introduction to each state are places to write for information on other, established trails.

This book was written in the hopes that, when the cares of the world weigh heavily on your spirit, you'll slip lightly onto your saddle, press your shoes into the silver toe clips, and pedal gracefully down a country road, enjoying the world as it was meant to be enjoyed—leisurely.

As one 75-year-old biker said, he liked cycling because "you see the scenery coming, you see it while it's there, and you see it going past."

Others may sweat and groan in the name of health, but you'll glide smoothly past urban and rural vistas, and return home refreshed and wiser, living proof of T. S. Eliot's observation:

"We shall not cease from exploration, and the end of all our exploring will be to arrive where we started, and know the place for the first time."

2

The Bike

You know you're hooked on biking when your first question, after hearing that your best buddy has been in an accident, is, "Was he riding the Cinelli?"

Not all people who enjoy biking value their machines over flesh and blood, however. And you don't have to own an expensive, hand-crafted cycle to have a good time. But if you plan to tour more than once or twice (and after once or twice, you'll plan to tour more often), you should invest in a 10-speed bike.

The specialized riding position of this cycle may seem awkward at first, but it has many advantages. It distributes your weight more evenly on your arms and legs, and puts your thigh and stomach muscles to work in pedaling. It prevents all the road shock from being absorbed by your seat and spine, and allows your legs to function more efficiently. It cuts wind resistance, which at speeds of over 14 miles an hour, accounts for 50 percent of your work. Once you get used to

Any kind of bike will do for short, day trips: 10-speeds, smaller bikes for the kids, or old-style balloon-tired bikes.

it, leaning forward on the bike becomes as natural as shifting gears in your car. You'll appreciate the greater control and efficiency such a position gives, and on trips of more than 10 miles, will find you get less fatigued than when using the upright riding position.

How do you choose your 10-speed from the hundreds of models on the market? The quality and type of bike you buy is a personal choice. Some bikes have freewheel and chain wheel sprockets designed for racing, others for climbing mountains. Racing frames can weigh less than four pounds and be made of bamboo poles. Obviously they are lightweight but very fragile. And some 10-speeds weigh a hefty 28 pounds or more.

Most bike frames are made out of tubing that resembles a gas pipe. Cheap tubing has to be thick in order for it to be strong. Thus a well made cheap bike will be heavy. If you tour a lot, or take mountain trips, where every ounce of weight means more work for you, you may be willing to pay for a lighter bike.

Lighter weight bikes can be stronger than heavier bikes, if aluminum alloys and certain specialized techniques in the manufacturing of the frame are used. These bikes are generally more expensive. Columbus, Reynolds 531, and Falk double-butted tubing make good bikes. As you go up in price and the bike gets lighter, you hope that it's as strong as that cheap, well-made bike.

Unfortunately, it's really not that simple. You can also get stuck with an expensive bike that's made with poor quality tubing, which is known as being "had."

There are also very well made, light racing bikes that are extremely fragile. They perform well, put the rider's energy where it's supposed to be, and bend the instant an inexperienced rider hits a pothole the wrong way.

Some people feel your bike should be as light and as well-constructed as you can possibly afford. Others say the hardware store variety 10-speed is fine for Midwestern bike trips. You don't put a lot of strain on the frame climbing steep mountains, and it's easy to get replacement parts for brand name bikes in smaller towns. When looking for a bike, your best bet is to find someone you trust who knows what he's talking about when he talks bikes.

Chat with friends who own 10-speeds and see what they like and dislike about their models. Check out the latest consumer report guides to see what's recommended. Borrow a friend's bike (if he'll lend it to you), and see how it rides.

Then find a bike dealer you trust. In some cases this means becoming an interviewer and people expert. Ask friends which bike shop they like, and why, and then get the name of the person at the shop they think is best. Many shops have one person who knows about everything from sprocket sizes to the latest French brakes, and another who can't tell a cotter pin from a gear shift lever. Some salesmen sound very authoritative but don't know what they're talking about when it comes to bikes. Ask a lot of questions and listen to their answers; eventually you'll find someone who makes sense. Tell the salesman what you want the bike for and see what he recommends and why. Think about your personal preferences, what your wallet can endure, and then make your purchase.

Give yourself time to break in your new bike. Don't dash off on a month's tour of the Great Lakes shoreline the day after you uncrate it. You need time to adjust to it, as well as to adjust it to you.

Buy toe clips and straps if they don't come with the bike. They make pedaling uphill much easier and aren't as hard to get used to as they look. If getting off the bike quickly worries you, leave the straps loose at first; eventually you'll become secure enough to tighten them.

BIKE SHOPS

If you plan to have your bike overhauled before leaving on tour (and you should plan to), but don't have the expertise to do it yourself, be nosy about who will repair your bike. To save money, sometimes bike shops hire people who love to practice fixing bikes. Beware that they don't practice on yours before you leave.

TIRES

After choosing a frame, consider what kind of tires to buy. Tires and saddle will be included in the purchase price of most hardware store variety 10-speeds. If the tires are 85 pounds, they're fine for touring. Less pressure is OK for short trips under 25 miles. For trips lasting several days, a higher pressure tire will reduce road friction and make pedaling easier. On tour, check your tires daily. Brush off any loose glass and gravel that may be on them, to prevent such junk from working its way into the tire and puncturing your tube. Also keep the tires filled with the proper pounds of air pressure.

If you buy new tires, you'll have to decide between 'sew-ups' and 'clinchers.'

A clincher tire is much like those found on cars and coaster brake bikes, with a thick outer tire and a thin inner tube. The tire rim is grooved and the tire "bead" fits into the groove. When the tire is filled with air, the bead pushes against the groove and holds the tire onto the rim.

There is no bead on the rim of a sew-up tire. The tire is glued onto the rim to keep it in place.

The original advantages of sew-ups were high pressure and light weight. At one time, the highest pressure clincher tire you could buy was 65 pounds; sew-ups hold up to 120 pounds. But in the last few years clincher tires have come out that hold up to 100 pounds.

And while bikers look for lightweight gear, the lightweight sew-up doesn't stand up to the punishment of gravel, sand, and rough roads; it is vulnerable to punctures, leaks, rim damage, and spoke breakage.

Many riders with top quality sew-ups now use lightweight clincher tires for rugged duty and reserve the sew-ups for special rides, or for racing. They buy 27-inch rims that can be used with either type tire.

The disadvantage of sew-ups is that they are actually sewn together on the inside of the tire. If you get a flat, you have to rip off the glued tire from the rim, tear out the sewn up section, pull out the tube, repair it, put it back into the tire, sew up the tire and then reglue it to the rim.

If you ride only on good surfaces such as racing tracks and never hit any potholes, sew-ups can last a long time. But most people don't need sew-ups. If you put a rack and 10 pounds on your bike, it's not a racing bike, so why bother with the racing tire?

Clincher tires are sold in more places than sew-ups. This is an important consideration in buying a tire, for you want something you can replace at the hardware store in Prairie Flats, U.S.A., if need be.

Before leaving for a several-day tour, check your tires and replace worn tires and tubes. The 85-pound-pressure tire is a favorite with bike trippers, but take along tire irons; high pressure tires can be hard to remove if you get a flat.

SAFETY LEVERS

In the past few years a new device called safety levers has appeared on 10-speed handlebars. The levers, which extend more or less parallel to the top of the handlebar, are supposed to make braking easier. Since the favored relaxed biking position for most cyclists is to rest their hands atop the bars, they don't have to reach down to squeeze the brakes when they have these levers on the handlebars.

However, safety levers are made out of aluminum, and aluminum flexes. When you hit these brakes hard, the long aluminum arm flexes, and the power from your muscles, which is supposed to go to the rim of the tire and squeeze it with the rubber brake bads, is lost.

Unless the levers are kept in fine adjustment, your braking efficiency is greatly reduced. To use these levers effectively, your wheels must be true, with no wobbles, and the brakes must be set tight.

If you like to brake from above, buy the expensive, but good quality, French Guidonnet brake handles, or set your brake handles high on the bars. Don't use safety levers, because they're not safety levers.

SADDLES

A new leather bike saddle is one of the hardest things to get used to. It may feel like you're sitting on a frying pan when you first buy one, yet in the long run, leather is superior to foam or vinyl saddles. If you bike a lot, trade in your plastic saddle for a leather one. After a few hundred miles of use, the leather will soften and conform somewhat to your shape. It is the most comfortable ride you can get on a bike.

Three complaints about leather saddles are, they're expensive, they're uncomfortable when you buy them, and you can't get them wet.

Some people recommend beating your new leather saddle

with a lead pipe to break it in. Others find rubbing Vaseline or neat's-foot oil on the underside of the saddle works out the hardness. Or you can break in a saddle by riding it every day for an hour. After a month of such a workout, you'll be used to the saddle and in shape to tackle a long tour as well.

Leather saddles *are* expensive, but in this case, you get what you pay for.

Keep an empty plastic bread bag in your tool kit and cover the saddle when it rains. If leather is abused extensively, dryness, cracking, loss of elasticity and other terrible things happen to it. Covering your saddle when you transport the bike on your car keeps off splattering insects as well as moisture.

One biker keeps his saddle in his car when he drives to a biking area. Now he's trying to figure out how to get the kids on the roof so he can put the whole bike in the back seat.

LOCKS

A six-foot cable, ¼ to ⁵/16 of an inch thick, and a shackle the size of a combination lock is best for touring, especially if there is more than one biker. Such a cable easily locks four bikes together.

Don't take a heavy Kryptonite lock. Most of the time you'll be near your bikes, whether you leave them in front of a restaurant or chain them around the tree by your tent.

TOOLS AND OTHER ACCESSORIES

The more a biker knows how to use a tool, the less likely he is to need it, because he's used it before he's left. The complete novice, who doesn't know how to use bike tools, can have a Snap-On tool truck follow him, and if his bike breaks down, it won't do him any good.

Repairing a bike on the side of the road while your

companions wait can take the fun out of biking. Just as you don't carry spare spark plugs or fan belts in your glove compartment, don't overload your bike repair kit. Major repairs should be taken care of before leaving home.

After your bike is overhauled, ride it several times to be sure the spokes, cones, and other parts work properly. Sometimes parts change their setting slightly after you ride, and have to be readjusted. If this is too confusing, have your bike work done in a reliable shop, ride it for three or four days, and if it makes any funny clunking or ca-chunking noises, take it back and tell them about it.

You won't normally take spoke wrenches or chain punches along on a one-day trip because you can rely on a well-cared-for bike holding up for a day. No major breakdowns should occur, and, as a rule of thumb, fewer tools are necessary on short trips. Some biking pros know their machines so well they can adjust spokes with a belt buckle if they have to.

On a one-day trip, don't plan for all catastrophes, just for those things that are most likely to happen. Cables break, tires go flat, and derailleurs need minor adjustments if they throw off the chain. For a one-day trip, take the bare minimum and keep other stuff like lubricant, cone wrenches, etc., in the car trunk, if you feel better with them nearby.

For a One-Day Trip

To repair a flat you need:

> Spare inner tube
> Tire irons
> Patch kit
> Valve gauge
> Air pump
> Adjustable wrench

To adjust a derailleur you need:

> Screwdriver, 6-inch

To keep your leather saddle dry you need:

> Empty plastic bread bag

To replace a cable you need:

> Pliers (to cut it)
> Spare rear brake cable

You need more tools for a longer trip, but don't bring along the whole tool chest. No matter how much you take, you'll find something you need that you didn't bring along. Such inconveniences make a trip challenging, and give you a chance to use your resourcefulness and self-reliance. Such was the case when a biking buddy bent his crank handle on a trip. Of all things, we could have used a hammer then. Instead, we pounded the crank back into shape with a log and large rock. Primitive tools, but they got him back home.

For a Two-Day Trip (or Longer)

Take everything you need for a one day trip plus:

> Lightweight oil (for lubricating your chain and cables)
> Bike rack (fastened to back wheel)
> Four bungi cords (21-inch) to fasten sleeping bag, tent and mat to your rear bike rack atop pannier bags (Criss-cross them to make a neat stable package, and you won't hear your tent poles bouncing down the road behind you.)
> Bike light, square battery-operated model that sits in a plastic clip on your handlebars and can be removed and used as a flashlight at night (Avoid generator lights—you don't need the extra work!)
> French arm-band light (for extra visibility on dreary days, in tunnels and fog)
> Chain punch and spare links

Optional:

> Spare brake pads (You won't wear them out on flat
> terrain, but if you forget to check them, they
> could work loose and fall out.)
> Three spokes and spoke wrench (Wheels flex, and
> spoles break. Unless you have excellent quality
> spokes and rims, the more weight you put on a
> bike, the more likely the spokes will break.)
> Freewheel remover may be necessary for replacing
> spokes on the rear wheel

LUBRICATION

Sometimes it seems as if there are as many types of
lubricant as there are brands of cereals at the local supermarket. One foams up, and then congeals in the nooks and
crannies of your chain, another is an aerosol spray, a third, a
powder you "puff" onto your chain from a plastic bottle.
These are fascinating, but they all serve the same purpose, to
keep your chain running smoothly, and to prevent rust.

One biker, frustrated by the profusion of lubricants, never
carries any with him.

"You pay three times as much for an ounce of lubricant as
you pay for a quart of oil," he says. When his chain needs
oiling, he stops in a gas station and uses the leftover oil from
quart cans that people throw into the trash. "There's more oil
there than you'd ever need for your chain and brake cables,"
he says.

Such Spartanism is admirable, but most bikers are willing to
pay extra, and carry a small can of lubricant with them.

Lubricants break down into two basic categories, wet, or
oil-based, and dry. Dry lubricants don't pick up dirt, but some
wash off in the rain. Oil lubricants are just the opposite. They
weather excellently, but pick up dirt.

Unless your preference for dry lube is strong, and you use
something like molybdenum disulfide, which weathers well,
it's simpler to just oil your chain when it's dry. Don't spend

more time playing with your chain than you do riding the bike. Leave it on the bike until it gets 10,000 miles on it, then take it off and throw it away. If you go through sand, wash it down with WD-40 and wipe off the excess oil. The few dollars you pay for a new chain will cost less than playing with foams, aerosols and powder "puffs."

WHERE WILL YOU PUT ALL THIS STUFF?

In pannier bags. Practice packing. Put the heaviest things, such as tools, on the bottom. Hopefully you'll need them least often, and, by setting them in the bottom of the bag, you lower the bike's center of gravity, making riding easier and safer. After you pack the bags, ride around the neighborhood to be sure you have them weighted evenly.

3

The Rider

Now that your bike is in shape, consider what fuel it will use. You are the motor for this machine, and eating a balanced diet is important, not only to stay healthy, but to get you to your destination.

Few bike tours will take you very far from a grocery store, but distances seem longer on a bike than in a car. Not only are you going slower, but you are burning energy as you ride.

Take along quick snack foods such as oranges, apples and bananas when you can get them. Be careful where you pack such fruit, but don't let that stop you from buying them. The lift they give is worth the trouble. "Gorp," that popular outdoorsman's mix of raisins, peanuts, and chocolate candy, gets to be boring food after a few days and if you're working hard, the peanuts lay heavily in your stomach. Probably the best instant energy food is raisins, straight from the box.

If you eat in restaurants, be sure one exists for the important meals—breakfast, lunch, and supper. An ice cream

On warm days,
make sure
your bike is
equipped with
a water bottle.

parlor, root beer drive-in, or fruit stand are nice bonuses, if you happen upon them.

Water is the most thirst quenching drink; sweet liquids such as pop actually increase your thirst because they are sugary.

ON A ONE-DAY TRIP

It's more convenient to eat breakfast at home or on the road (if you are driving to a biking area) than to make it and take it along with you. Take a picnic lunch, and eat supper in a restaurant on the way home. Don't drag stoves, eating utensils, and other gear for three meals along on a one-day trip. Biking is your main focus, not making meals.

A nice biker's picnic lunch that doesn't spoil easily might

This bike camper knows how to travel light.

consist of cheese, salami or spicy meat, fresh fruit, candy bars for energy, and bagels, which don't mash, crumble, or rip. If possible, buy a bottle of orange juice before you stop for lunch; otherwise, drink from your water bottle.

Stay away from beer and other alcohols on lunch break. It makes you drowsy, as it decreases the oxygen-carrying ability of the blood. Pedaling in the afternoon will be harder and you'll be less alert. When biking is done in the evening, some people find beer or wine a pleasant way to relax. But if you've biked 50 miles, you'll be plenty relaxed without the alcohol.

Many bikers take chewing gum to keep their throat moist while they bike. Hard candy also keeps your mouth from getting dry; just don't laugh when you suck on it.

ON A TRIP OF SEVERAL DAYS

If you cook, plan your meals two days in advance, deciding

what you will eat, and making sure there is someplace to buy the food. On backroads, the only grocery is often a ma-pa type store where you can't be choosy about what you buy. Do check for edibility when you shop, making sure the bread is not moldy, or that the selling date on cheese, etc., has not passed.

Buy your groceries around 4 p.m., preferably just before a long, downhill run to your campsite. Make supper your big meal of the day so you can digest your food leisurely. By eating most of what you buy at your evening meal, you have less to carry the next morning.

Take an emergency meal. Something simple, like a package of macaroni and cheese, in case the restaurant you planned to have steak at doesn't exist anymore.

COOKING UTENSILS

Part of the delightfulness of touring is being close to nature and on your own, but it does require special, lightweight equipment.

Use a small, hot-burning stove to cook on, such as the Swedish SVEA, which is about five inches high by three inches in diameter. Take ½ liter of white gas for every week you'll cook out. This should be plenty for making breakfast and supper.

Take a six-inch-diameter aluminum pot, pan, and lid (a two-pint pot serves four cups of soup).

Each person should have his own small plastic cup, fork, knife, and spoon. I use a jacknife with a spoon attached to one side, and a fork to the other. You can't toss a salad with this fork and spoon combination, and they are small, but they work fine for camping. After biking all day, you aren't fussy about how you eat; even beer in a paper cup is inviting.

SHELTER

You can stay at lodges and motels, or you can camp.

Bike campers' tents should be light, but waterproof.

If you camp, you can sleep under the stars, but have a waterproof bag in case of rain. Better still, take along a tarp for warm weather, or a lightweight tent. Two-man tents as light as two pounds can be purchased. The major complaint against these tents, besides their expense, is that they don't breathe. After a night's use, they smell like a stable if not aired out.

There is a three-pound eight-ounce tent made of triple layer fabric that breathes, keeps out rain, and yet lets moisture from inside the tent escape. For information write:

> Light Dimensions Tents
> Early Winters, Ltd.
> 300 Queen Anne Avenue
> Seattle, Wash. 98109

Whatever tent you use, let it air out and dry in the

morning. Not only does this keep it from getting moldy, it makes a difference in the weight you carry on your bike.

Lightweight Dacron sleeping bags are good for most spring through fall weather. Two-pound bags are sold at most sports outlets. If you're sure the weather will be hot, grab a lightweight blanket off the bed, roll it in a plastic bag, and use it for summer camping.

Get a good mat for a good night's rest. Air mattresses tend to leak or puncture. Buy a camping mat, or purchase a double bed foam padding that is one inch thick. By cutting it lengthwise, you have two super-comfortable, lightweight mats. Such bed padding costs about half the price, per person, of a camping mat and is twice as comfortable.

If you have a well-padded wallet you can sleep on it in motels, but make reservations in advance and call to confirm them.

CLOTHING

This is a matter of personal choice. Start off with a small list and try to keep it that way.
Possible items:

> Hat with brim (to keep off rain and sun and to avoid heat prostration)
> One change of underwear and socks (Wash them out at night, and you'll always have a clean pair.)
> Shirt and shorts for biking (Polyester is nice; wash it at night, and even if it's not completely dry the next day, let it dry on your body. At least the old salt and sweat is out of it.)
> Longsleeve cotton shirt and long pants (for evening)
> Wool sweater
> Rain poncho
> Sneakers, or other shoes (If you wear biking shoes, you'll need something to walk in, for even the

canvas beta biking shoes give blisters on long hikes.)
Swimsuit

Most museums, restaurants, and places of entertainment accept casual dress nowadays, as long as you pay the admission price. If you need more clothes, you can buy them on the road.

Keep an extra pair of wool socks in your sleeping bag for spring and fall biking. Warm, dry socks at night are a real comfort if your feet are cold or wet.

LUXURIES AND PERSONAL ITEMS MIGHT INCLUDE:

Camera
Sunglasses
Lip ointment or skin cream
Suntan lotion
Insect repellent
Soap, comb
Toothbrush, toothpaste
Washcloth and small towel

FIRST AID

The best first aid is to stay out of accidents. If you do have a small mishap, it's nice to have some disinfectant and an adhesive bandage along. Most commercial first aid kits never seem to have exactly what you want, and too much of what you'd never think of using. And they're bulky to carry. Make up your own kit by taking an empty plastic prescription pill bottle, one inch in diameter by two inches in length, or an empty 35 mm film cannister. For a weekend trip, put the following in it:

Band-Aids (2-3) and pack a small tube of disinfec-
tant cream in your pannier
Several aspirins
Small piece of moleskin (to prevent blisters)
One or two nasal or cold tablets

A clean handkerchief serves as an emergency bandage, and
for longer trips, add a small roll of one-half-inch adhesive
tape (also good for taping parts of the bike that may need first
aid) and several two-inch squares of sterile gauze.

4

Problems, Solutions, and Safety

Good planning makes for good endings, so before you leave, decide how you will get back to your car after biking. If your route circles back to where you parked the car, you have no problem. Just load your bikes onto the auto and drive home.

But sometimes scenic countryside, good roads and points of interest can be best appreciated only on a linear trip. You may choose to follow the route of a river, the shoreline of one of the Great Lakes, or a back road that takes you 50 miles or more from the place where you leave your car.

Several listings in this book are such linear trips. That is, they don't end up where they started. If you take a linear trip, there are several ways to get back to your car. Such as:

—Retrace your path and bike back via the road you came.

—Take a bus, train, or plane back to the place you left the car, if these services are available.

—Someone who doesn't intend to bike can follow you, driving a sag wagon. A variant of the sag wagon is to have

The logistics of getting your bikes to the starting point can be complicated.

the bikers themselves drive the car in shifts. This variant is never popular, however, because bikers are a nutty lot who, when they take a 300-mile bike trip, want to cover each of the 300 miles on their bikes. They believe the whole idea of bike camping is to become independent of the auto.

CAR SHUTTLE

—Another method of getting back to your car is the shuttle, also called "spotting your car." Made popular by canoeists, the shuttle is now a standard method used to get bikers and cars together at the end of a trip.

A shuttle seems simple enough. Just drive one of the cars down to where you'll end the trip so it'll be waiting when you arrive. Yet it's surprising how many people haven't thought the shuttle maneuvers through. You need at least two cars for the shuttle, which has five basic steps.

1) Drive cars A and B to starting point and unload gear.

2) Leave someone to watch the bikes and gear, while two drivers take cars A and B to the place you'll end your trip. Park car B in a safe place at the end and lock it. Both drivers return in car A to the starting point.

3) Park car A in a safe place and lock it at the starting point.

4) Bike your route.

5) At the end of the trip car B is waiting for you. Two drivers take car B back to the starting point and pick up car A. Drive both cars to the end and pick up the rest of the bikers.

A car shuttle works well for trips where the road to be driven (which is not necessarily the road to be biked) is under 50 miles, or whenever the driving time is less than an hour, from beginning to ending point. Remember, you have to drive to the ending point and back, which doubles the time spent in your car both at the beginning and at the end of your trip.

There is an alternative method of getting back to your car when you take a trip of over 50 miles, with a half-dozen or more people. Before leaving, divide the party into two groups which will bike in opposite directions along the same route. Plan to meet in the center of the trip at a well-marked location—campsite, restaurant, or museum. You may be waiting an hour or more so don't pick a telephone pole next to a deserted junction as a meeting spot.

Each group parks and locks its car on opposite ends of the route, and bikes towards the middle. Figure in advance how long the trip will take (an average of 10 miles an hour is OK if you add time for steep hills, lunch stops, sights, rests, etc.). Find the "time" center of the trip, which differs from the mileage center of the trip. The "time" center is the place where it will take you just as long to get to either end of the route.

Choose a landmark to meet at, a place you can leave messages for each other, and an approximate meeting time. When both groups meet there, exchange car keys and locations (be specific about where you left the car), and continue on your respective journeys. At the end of the trip each party takes the other group's car and drives to a previously agreed upon place to pick up their own cars.

DOGS

You may love man's best friend, but on a bike, all dogs, even your own, can be dangerous. During one trip through the Illinois countryside, my own dog ran in front of my wheel after a rabbit, toppling me and the bike. After being upended, I ended up with scraped palms and elbows and sore knees. My bike suffered a bent rim, sand in its crank, broken spokes, and other bruises. I still bike with my dog on occasion, but now I keep close watch and expect him to do the unexpected.

Perhaps I would have been safer had he been a strange dog, for then I would have been ready for trouble. When biking, defensive riding is the best precaution against dogs and other dangers.

If you have young children biking with you, tell them before you begin what to expect if they come upon a dog, and what to do. Dogs bark, chase bikes, and occasionally jump on or bite bikers. The best way to handle a dog is to stay cool. This is tough advice to follow as you stare into those menacing jaws with the sharp white canines gleaming near your calves, but very often it works.

When a dog chases your bike, yell in your deepest, most authoritative voice, "Go home!" Even if he doesn't listen, such a commanding tone will give you confidence. And you'll be amazed and gratified to see how many times such a command actually works. If you are a strong rider and don't have to worry about others in your party, you can try to outrun the beast. Most dogs tire more quickly than a biker, although they may have the edge at first. Also, if you bike far enough, you'll bike out of the dog's "territory," at which point he'll lose interest in the chase. If you're going downhill, you have an advantage, but be careful that you don't ride out of control, which can be just as dangerous as being attacked by a dog.

Man's best friend is probably best left at home when you take a bike trip.

Some bikers swing their air pumps at the dog, trying to hit it on the nose, where it will smart the most. Just the sight of a pump will sometimes discourage dogs. However, swinging a weapon while biking can be awkward and if you're not careful, can throw you off balance. Hitting a dog in such a manner can also ruin your tire pump.

Other bikers carry a stinging solution made up of two parts water to one part ammonia in a squeezable plastic bottle. They keep it in a handlebar pack where it is easily accessible. When a dog threatens, they squirt it at his face.

Or you can get off the bike and walk it, keeping it between you and the dog. I personally feel that whatever advantage I have is lost by getting off the bike, unless I'm going uphill. But anything that works is a good defense against dogs.

TRUCKS AND CARS

Ride as far to the right of the road as is reasonable and safe. When you hear a car approaching from behind, yell "car!" to the biker ahead of you to give him warning. If you are riding with younger children, always have an adult follow them who can warn them of approaching vehicles and shepherd them to the side of the road when they drift too far into the lane.

Semi-trucks are extremely dangerous. The force of the wind alone when they pass at high speeds is enough to knock you off the road. Stay off roads where they will be traveling at high speeds. To avoid big, speeding trucks, look for secondary roads, or ones that are posted with the warning, "5 ton limit."

WEATHER

There is no such thing as bad weather, only different kinds of good weather. You can bike in hot, sunny weather, in cold, brisk weather, and even in invigorating rain, if you follow some common sense rules. Biking through a light rain can be a refreshing experience, as long as you are on level ground or climbing a hill. Biking downhill in the rain is hazardous, as it will take at least twice as long to brake as it would in dry weather.

If there is lightning, stay off your bike. If you do ride in the rain, wear a brightly colored poncho to increase your visibility.

Cool weather makes pleasant biking if you're dressed warmly. Your body generates heat, so you won't shiver if you wear a windbreaker or jacket that keeps in body heat and keeps out cool breezes. If you cycle in weather that's downright nippy, wear extra wool socks and gloves to keep your fingers and toes warm.

In hot weather, wear a hat to prevent sunburn and heat exhaustion, take suntan lotion, and a long sleeve cotton shirt for later in the day. Stop to rest often, and drink plenty of water.

SAFETY

Always ride with traffic, not against it, and ride single file on the shoulder if it is paved, or as close to it as is safe, if it's not paved. The two biggest dangers for bikers are riding on the wrong side of the road, and not paying attention at intersections.

In the city, watch for opening doors of parked cars, or you may find yourself hanging over one. Use standard hand signals for all stops and turns, and yield the right of way to pedestrians or anything bigger than you are. Gravel, sand, and metal grates placed lengthwise along a street curb are other biking dangers to watch for.

States have varying laws for cyclists. Check the chapter introductions in this book for current legislation in the state you bike through. For further information on laws regarding bikers, write the Secretary of State in the capital city of the state, or contact:

Edward Kearney
National Committee for Uniform Traffic Laws
1776 Massachusetts Avenue, N. W.
Suite 4300
Washington, D. C. 20036
phone: 202/785-4066

5

Illinois: Introduction and Trails

State Capital: Springfield
State Flower: Native Violet
State Tree: White Oak
State Bird: Cardinal
State Nickname: "Prairie State"

Just outside Chicago, there's a place called Illinois that is rich in history and farmland. A tour through any part of it is sure to prove educational as well as enjoyable. The primarily level land makes for relaxed family biking and every county maintains a historical society or museum which focuses on its special contribution to the state.

Originally, 42 percent of the land in this state was forest, but lumbering reduced that to less than 6 percent today. Much of Illinois is a patchwork quilt of farmland with tractors furrowing it in the spring and harvesting in fall.

There are no mountains in this state, but there are areas

Cook County's Botanic Garden is a spectacular sight in spring.

where the landscape dips and climbs and offers bikers stiff hills and bluffs. These regions are in the northwest corner of the state near Galena; at the southern tip, in what is called the Illinois Ozarks; and along the Mississippi River, where rugged bluffs carved by the river are part of several state parks.

Though the terrain is mostly flat, the history and personality of the state has many contours. Ride through quiet rural areas near the Wisconsin border, visit frontier forts in the middle of the state, or bike to English and French villages and pioneer towns along the Mississippi River.

The really adventurous cyclist can follow the Mississippi

River the length of the state and then bike back north through the center of it, passing through rich historical cities such as New Salem, Lincoln, and the capital, Springfield.

In Chicago, you'll crane your neck to see some of the highest skyscrapers in the world, or watch the bustle of the city from its lakeshore bike path.

Even before white settlers brought their civilization to the state, Illinois had a cultural history. More than 10,000 Indian mounds from various cultures have been found here. One of the richest archeological areas in the Midwest is in Fulton County at the junction of the Spoon and Illinois rivers. A museum has been erected near Lewistown on a high bluff overlooking the two rivers, on Dickson mound.

Watch on-going archaeological excavations at the on-site museum in Cahokia State Park, or journey through the beautiful Rock River area and visit Black Hawk State Park, which commemorates the Sauk Indians' last stand in Illinois with a museum and Labor Day weekend Indian pow-wow.

In central Illinois, visit the Amish villages near the towns of Arcola and Arthur. Share the quiet backroads with clip-clopping horses pulling Amish buggies, and watch bearded farmers dressed in black work their fields with horse-drawn implements. Saturday is the best time to visit the Amish settlements, and horse auctions are held at the Arthur Sale Barn on the fourth Saturday of the month. Saturday is also market day, when farmers sell fruits and vegetables in season.

Near Belleville, the beautiful National Shrine of Our Lady of the Snows is the largest outdoor devotional site in North America.

At Nauvoo, a town founded along the Mississippi River by the Mormons, you can participate in the annual wine festival, "The Wedding of Wine and Cheese," a celebration which began with the town's French population during the late 1800s. The winding trail along the Mississippi River offers many panoramic views in the area.

County fairs are rich in Illinois. Springfield has the State Fair in August, which draws over a million visitors from

Chicago's lakefront bike path is a great way to see the Windy City.

several states. At the Fort Massac 1776 Festival, colonial militia man the fort, and bikers can watch local artisans perform crafts. For dates and information on this and other events, write for the booklet, *Calendar of Events,* at:

Illinois Office of Tourism
222 South College Street
Springfield 62706

The Office of Tourism can also send you an *Illinois Camping Guide,* and an *Illinois Motel and Hotel Directory.*

Though Illinois has 5.5 percent of the nation's population, half its people live in the northeast corner of the state, in and around Chicago.

Yet a bike trip through this hulking city can be a relaxing experience. Foresighted city planners allowed for a lakefront of largely unspoiled parks. You can bike along the lake through most of Chicago on a bike path, or cycle on pleasant, cool paths that wind through the vast forest preserve district encompassing the northern, western, and southern parts of the city and its suburbs.

For a map, and a list of architecturally significant homes along a bike path, write:

> Chicago School of Architecture Foundation
> Glessner House
> 1800 South Prairie Avenue
> Chicago 60616
> phone: 312/326-1393

For trails through the North Branch of the Forest Preserve, write:

> North Branch Division Headquarters
> Forest Preserve
> 6633 Harms Road
> Niles 60206
> phone: 312/326-1393

A pamphlet, *Illinois Bike Trails,* which lists 18 scenic trips throughout the state, ranging in length from 6 to 240 miles, is available from:

> The Illinois Adventure Center
> 160 North LaSalle Street
> Room 100
> Chicago 60601

A large scale, detailed Illinois Official Highway Map that is published annually can be had for free by writing:

> Division of Highways
> 2300 South 31st Street
> Springfield 62706

For information on the 25 mile *Illinois Prairie Path,* which starts in Elmhurst, a Chicago suburb, and follows the former Chicago, Aurora and Elgin railroad right of way across DuPage and Kane counties, write:

> Illinois Prairie Path
> Box 1086
> 616 Delles Road
> Wheaton 60187
> phone: 312/665-5310

For a map and information on the Moraine State Park bike trail write:

> Site Superintendent
> Moraine State Park
> 914 South River Road
> McHenry 60050
> phone: 815/385-1624

For information on other Illinois State Parks, write:

> Department of Conservation
> Land and Historic Sites
> State Office Building
> Springfield 62706

For a map-brochure of the Chicago area bike paths, write:

> Chicago Park District
> 425 East McFetridge Drive
> Chicago 60605
> phone: 312/294-2200

The American Youth Hostels puts out a pamphlet called

Chicago Area Cycle Routes, giving 14 trails of from 20 to 90 miles in the Chicago area. Write:

> American Youth Hostels
> Chicago Metropolitan Council
> 3172 North Clark Street
> Chicago 60613
> phone: 312/327-8114

To obtain detailed county maps of Illinois, write:

> Bureau of Planning
> Division of Highways
> Department of Public Works and Buildings
> Springfield 62706
> (½ inch = 1 mile. 50¢ a map.)

For information on a 60 mile tour through the Spoon River Valley, write:

> Spoon River Bikeway
> Spoon River Scenic Drive Association
> Box 59
> Ellisville 61431

For information on a ten mile, North Shore bike trail, which connects to the 18 mile Chicago lakefront path, write:

> Green Bay Trail
> Box 47
> Hubbard Woods 60093

To find out where to take a 20 mile bike trail through forest preserves west of Chicago, write:

> Cook County Forest Preserves
> 536 North Harlem Avenue
> River Forest 60305

ILLINOIS BIKE RULES

In Illinois, bikers must obey all vehicle regulations, street and highway signs, and must use hand signals for stops and turns. Stop for school buses, and ride in single file with other cyclists. When a bicycle path has been provided, use it.

GALENA AND TWO STATE PARKS

You realize the notion that Illinois is all flat is a myth as you climb up and coast down plenty of hills on this trip in the northwest part of the state. In addition to the rolling countryside, three areas that combine geological and historical points of interest are the Mississippi Palisades State Park, just north of Savanna; Apple River Canyon State Park; and Galena, a city proud of its rich heritage.

Glaciers, which leveled the plains in most of Illinois, left this corner of the state untouched. The area around Galena was also once rich in lead mines, which Father Marquette saw Indians work with primitive tools. By the 1800s, Galena, which means "lead sulphide," was a boom lead-mining town and port city. But the mines were shallow and the new railroad stole away the river traffic, so Galena's population shrank, until it became known as the "city that time forgot." More than 50 buildings, which were built between 1820 and 1880, still stand in the town. They are situated on the town's five levels, which include streets that challenge the climbing abilities of the most expert biker.

Spend a morning, or take an extra day to leisurely enjoy the restored historical buildings, which include two state memorials, the Ulysses S. Grant home, and the Old Market House. See the underground hiding rooms of the Underground Railroad, specialty museums, 25 antique shops, many gift and art galleries. Ride six miles out of town to see the Vinegar Hill Lead Mine, or take a river excursion on the Mississippi River aboard a stern-wheel boat.

The first day, leave your car in Elizabeth, a town 13 miles southeast of Galena, and bike the round trip of 44 miles to

Savanna. The first 10 miles have two long and challenging hills. Just outside Savanna stop at the Mississippi Palisades State Park and view the island-dotted river from atop towering limestone cliffs. The park also has Indian mounds and strangely shaped rock formations.

If you carry your lunch, eat at the Palisades State Park, or enjoy a leisurely meal at one of several Savanna restaurants, just a few miles south of the park. After lunch retrace your path to Elizabeth, and shuttle cars and bikes to Galena for sightseeing and an overnight stay, either at lodges or campgrounds. The distance between Elizabeth and Galena is only 13 miles, but five of those miles are on a busy section of route 20, with heavy truck traffic, something all living bikers avoid.

Make an early departure from Galena on the second day, and bike some 30 miles east to the Apple River Canyon State Park. Ride on the Old Stagecoach Trail from Galena to the town of Warren. The hilly, scenic route passes within several miles of Charles Mound, the highest point in Illinois, at 1,235 feet.

At Warren, take route 78 south four miles to the paved road that turns west into Apple River Canyon State Park. Have lunch at the park and return to Galena via the same route.

WHEN TO GO:

Spring through fall. Galena offers many special events throughout the year. Plan your trip in time to see one of them.

In mid-May, the U.S. Grant Civil War Cantonment re-enacts Civil War battles, has bowie knife and tomahawk throwing contests, a musket shoot, military ball, parade, and other festivities.

During the second full week of June, an Open House and Farmer's Market is held.

In mid-June, the town puts on an arts and crafts festival.

The last week in September, an annual tour of historic Galena homes is held. This is also a time when the hills are brilliant with autumn color.

LOCATION:
Northwest corner of Illinois. Jo Daviess and Carroll counties.

TERRAIN:
Hilly.

TRAVEL:
100 miles. You make two round trips; a 44 mile round trip from Elizabeth to Savanna is the first. Then shuttle 13 miles from Elizabeth to Galena on a busy highway. The second round trip is about 60 miles, from Galena to the Apple River Canyon State Park.

ROAD SURFACE:
Paved, unless you decide to bike the 13 miles between Elizabeth and Galena. Here there is about 15 miles of gravel travel. The gravel is well-packed, but roads are narrow, so watch out for cars that come blazing up the other side of the hills.

TYPE OF TOUR:
Day, tour, or camp.

ROUTE:
Day one. Begin in Elizabeth. Take route 20 west 3 miles to 84, south 20 miles to Savanna. Retrace 84 north 20 miles to 20, east 3 miles to Elizabeth.

Day two. Begin in Galena. Take Old Stagecoach Trail 23 miles east and north to Warren. 78 south 5 miles to Apple River Canyon Road, west 2 miles to the Park. Retrace Park Road east 2 miles to 78, north 5 miles to Warren. Old Stagecoach Trail 23 miles south and west to Galena.

CAMPING:
Palace Campground, 2 miles west of Galena on 20. Showers, swimming, store, snack bar, pool, horseback riding. 815/777-2466.

Wooded Wonderland. 5 miles east of Galena on 20. 300 sites. Showers, boat rental, swimming, store. 815/777-1223.

Apple River Canyon State Park. 100 sites. Store, snack bar, hiking. 815/745-3302.

Lakewood Resort. 100 sites. Mill Hollow Road, 5 miles north of Savanna on 84. Showers, swimming, snack bar, store.

Mississippi Palisades State Park. 350 sites. Showers, store hiking, year-round interpretive program. 815/273-2731.

INFORMATION:

Galena Chamber of Commerce, 124 N. Main Street, 61036. 815/777-0203.

Savanna Chamber of Commerce, Box 315, 61074.

LODGING:

Chestnut Mountain Lodge, Blackjack Road, Galena. 815/777-1320.

De Soto Hotel and Bar, 230 S. Main St., Galena. 815/777-9208.

Grant Hills Motel, Hwy 20 E., 815/777-2116.

RESTAURANTS:

Gen. Grant's Traveling Rations, 205 Main, Galena. 815/777-1531. Daily except Wed. 10:30 a.m.–6:30 p.m.

Raleigh's, 300 N. Main St., 815/777-0451. Daily except Thurs. 11:30-1 p.m., 6–9:30 p.m.

Other restaurants in Galena and Savanna.

BIKE CARE:

Bussans Village Hardware in Galena, 815/777-0983.

Coast-To-Coast Store in Savanna, 815/273-3970.

TRANSPORTATION:

Bus and train to Galena. Bus to Savanna. Air service to Dubuque and Clinton, Iowa.

Galena Bike Trip Map

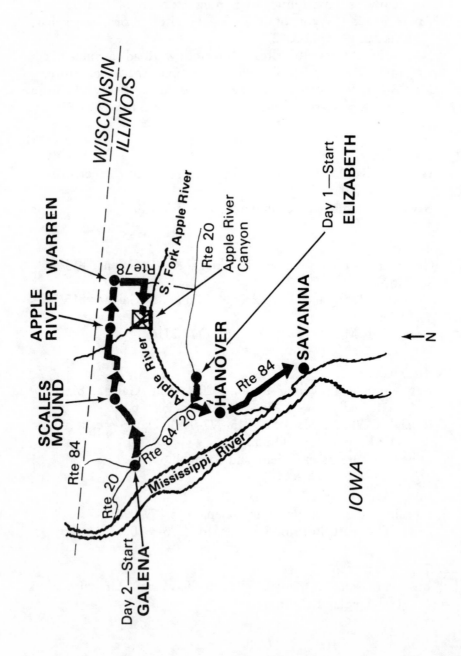

ROCKFORD, ILLINOIS, TO LAKE GENEVA, WISCONSIN*

Once out of the Chicago megalopolis, Northern Illinois is pleasantly rural, with soft, rolling hills and tree canopied roads. This 100 mile trip from Rockford, Illinois, to Lake Geneva, Wisconsin, and back can be done in a day by the seasoned pedaler. Or make it a weekend trip and stay overnight in the resort town of Lake Geneva.

Rockford is the second largest city in Illinois, with huge industrial plants covering its southern areas, but the northern portion of the city on up into Wisconsin is good biking. Named for a shallow, rock-bottomed ford that the Chicago-Galena stagecoach used to cross the Rock River, the city has a rich Scandinavian heritage. Visit the Erlander Home Museum at 404 S. Third Street, built in 1871, that is maintained by the Swedish Historical Society. The 26-room Tinker Swiss Cottage, built in 1865 at 311 Kent Street, is also open to the public and can be reached by crossing a suspension bridge across Kent Creek.

North of Rockford, located between Highways 41 and 90, is Rock Cut State Park, which, combined with Pierce Lake, serves as a recreation area.

At the other end of your trip, in Wisconsin, Lake Geneva is a clean, picturesque resort town along a sparkling lake. It's a good place to stop for a swim, to shop, to eat, or to stay overnight.

LOCATION:
Northern Illinois and southern Wisconsin in counties Winnebago, Boone, and McHenry in Illinois, and Walworth and Rock counties in Wisconsin.

TERRAIN:
Hilly.

---

*Route courtesy of Fred Kennerly, Blackhawk Bicycle Club in Rockford.

TRAVEL:
100 miles.

TIME:
1-2 days.

ROAD SURFACE:
Paved.

TYPE OF TRIP:
Day, tour, or camp.

ROUTE:
Begin at the North Towne Mall on Main Street in Rockford. Main St north to Frontage Rd, north and west to Elmwood, west to Rockton Av, north to Latham Rd, east to Old River Rd, north to Gleasman Rd, northeast to Roscoe Rd, northeast to Main St (Roscoe), north to Chestnut St, east to Burr Oak Rd, east to Crockett, north to Elevator, east to Town Line Rd, north to Manchester, east to Free Church Rd, north to State Line Rd, west and north to Beloit Rd, northeast to County Rd W (east into Sharon) to County Rd B, east (out of Sharon) to Six Corners Rd, north (into Walworth) to Beloit Rd (Kenosha St), east to 67, north and east to Fontana Blvd, east to South Shore Drive, south and east to County Rd BB, south and west to County Rd B, west (into Walworth) to Beloit Rd (Kenosha St), west to County B, west to County J, west to County P, south and west to Beloit Rd, south and west to State Line Rd, south and west to Willowbrook Rd, south to Rockton Rd, west to East Union St, west to Blackhawk St (Route 75), south to Russell, south and east to Old River Rd, south to Gleasman St.

WHEN TO GO:
Summer through fall.

Even the smallest tots—like this youngster—can enjoy a bike trip.

CAMPING:

Rock Cut State Park. 5 miles north on U.S. 51, 2 miles east on Harlem Rd. 400 sites. Shower, store. Rockford.

Willow Wood, 4 miles south on U.S. 51 to bypass 20. 3½ miles south on U.S. 51. 2 miles west on Baxter Rd to 3509 S Bend Rd. 200 sites. Showers, store. April 1–November 15. Rockford.

Oakey's Orchard. 5 miles north on U.S. 51. 1½ mile east on Harlem Rd. 200 sites. Showers, store. April 1–November 1. Rockford.

Oak Valley Campground. 4 miles south on U.S. 51. 1½ mile east on Blackhawk Rd. ¾ mile south on County R. 215 sites. Showers. Rockford.

Big Foot Beach State Park, Lake Geneva. 1 mile west on Hwy 120. 100 sites.

INFORMATION:

Rockford Chamber of Commerce, 815 E. State St., 61101. 815/987-8100.

Rockford to Lake Geneva, Wisconsin, Map

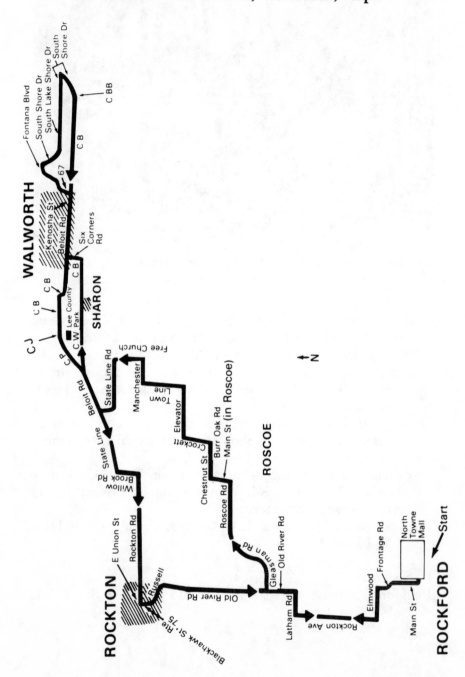

Lake Geneva area Chamber of Commerce, 100 Lake St., Lake Geneva, 53147. 414/248-4416.

LODGING:

Holiday Inn in Rockford. 4419 S. 11th St. at Samuelson Rd. 5 miles south on 51. Pool. 815/397-4000.

Motel 6. 4205 11th St. at Samuelson. Just west of 51. ¾ mile south of 20 bypass. 815/399-6266. Pool. Rockford.

Regal 8 Inn. 3851 11th St. 4 miles south on 51 at 20 bypass. 815/398-6080. Rockford.

Lake Geneva Motel. ¾ mile south on County H. Lake Geneva. 414/248-3464.

RESTAURANTS:

In Rockford: Bishop Buffet. S. Alpine Rd at Newberg Rd in the Colonial Village Shopping Center. 11 a.m.-7 p.m. 815/398-2123.

D'Agostino's. 4433 Charles. 4 miles southeast. 815/399-9546. Rockford.

Glen Nelson's. 812 Main St. at jct 36/50 off 12. Lake Geneva. 414/248-3571.

Silvano's. 1 mile north on County H. Lake Geneva. 414/248-8117.

BIKE CARE:

Geneva Cyclery. 414/248-9090. Lake Geneva.

Lakeland Firestone, Lake Geneva. 414/248-9133.

TRANSPORTATION:

Air service, bus, and train to Rockford.

JACKSONVILLE TO NEW SALEM*

Ride tall, you're in Lincoln country on this trip, and will bike through towns where honest Abe lived and worked as a

---

*Route courtesy of David Massey, Easy Riders Bicycle Club in Jacksonville.

circuit riding lawyer before he became President. Part of the tour is along the scenic and historic 2,200-mile, medallion-marked Lincoln Heritage Trail, which runs through Illinois, Indiana, and Kentucky. If you are interested, other parts of the Lincoln Heritage Trail are replete with forts, fairs, and festivals, and make worthwhile biking. Write the Division of Tourism in each state for information on the trail.

Illinoisans are proud of their Lincoln heritage and the historical high point of this trip comes when you visit New Salem, the reconstructed log village where Lincoln spent six years of his early adulthood, and where he reached a turning point in his life. Part of the charm of this village is its setting, which overlooks the Sangamon Valley.

Lincoln met Ann Rutledge at New Salem and lived here from 1831 to 1837. The log cabins have been restored to look as they did when Lincoln was elected to the legislature from Sangamon County in 1834. A seven-hour television special on pioneer life, "The Awakening Land: The Saga of an American Woman," which deals with the stalwart frontier woman, was filmed here in 1977 because of the authentic pioneer setting.

The admission-free site has 12 houses, Rutledge Tavern and shops, stores, sawmill, gristmill, and school. The only original structure is the Onstot cooper shop, built in 1835. Nevertheless, careful attention to authentic furnishings and landscaping give the village an aura of the past. Many articles on display were donated by families whose ancestors used them in the 1830s.

From May through October, on the third Sunday of each month, militia in full dress march off to the Black Hawk War, just as Lincoln did, and craft demonstrations of weaving, spinning, water witching, cooking, and horseshoeing are given by workers in pioneer dress. Almost every day from June through August, some type of crafts are demonstrated, including cooking in the Rutledge Tavern kitchen. A replica of a steamboat offers hour long trips in summer and fall.

The city of Jacksonville is in a lovely area in central

Illinois, and is where your trip begins. Before the Civil War, the city was an important station on the Underground Railroad.

East of the city the land is flat, with farms and many cornfields. West of Jacksonville are rolling hills and river valleys. This trip goes through farmland and very small farm villages, along river bluffs, and through the restored town of New Salem. If you like, take some extra time and travel the Lincoln Post Trail from New Salem 12 miles into Springfield, and visit the Capitol of Illinois.

Just before the town of Arenzville are some hills, with a steep drop into the town itself. From Arenzville to route 104, you ride along beautiful bluffs. There is a small section of busy highway travel along routes 67 and 104, but route 100 to Bluffs is lightly traveled. You ride on small bluffs along the Illinois River.

Just before the town of Bluff take a side trip into Naples, a river town where General Grant crossed the Illinois River with his troops. Grant's march from Springfield to Jacksonville to Naples is marked along the route. The Naples Inn serves good meals and you can look out over the river as you eat.

From the town of Bluff you climb a hill into the town of Exeter. This was an important town in the 1850–1880s, that almost died, but is coming back to life. The three story brick hotel there is restored.

The remainder of the route back to Jacksonville is farmland, with several cornfields and hog farms. This trip is one of the most scenic rides in central Illinois.

LOCATION:
Central Illinois in Morgan, Scott, Cass, Menard, and Sangamon counties.

TERRAIN:
Rolling farmland, some bluffs. North and west of Jacksonville, hilly with a few steep hills; east of Jacksonville, flat.

TRAVEL:
150 miles.

TIME:
2 to 4 days.

ROAD SURFACE:
Paved.

TYPE OF TRIP:
Tour or camp.

WHEN TO GO:
Spring through fall.

ROUTE:
Take Old State Road (CR 3) out of Jacksonville east 16 miles
to Berlin. Take CR 10 north 8 miles to Pleasant Plains.
Take only paved road north ½ mile, then east 3 miles,
then north 3 miles, then west ½ mile to 5, north 4 miles
to New Salem State Park Road entrance. After visiting
park, take 5 north 2 miles to 4, west 2 miles to 13, north
6½ miles to 7, 2 miles (Oakford) to 12, west 10 miles to
Chandlerville. Take 7 west 15 miles to Beardstown to 8,
south 10 miles to Arenzville. Take 11 west 8 miles to jct
100-104. Take 100 south 6 miles into Bluffs. Take 1 south
and east 4 miles to 36, east 5 miles to only paved county
road that jogs north and east back into Jacksonville.

CAMPING:
Lincoln's New Salem State Historical Site, New Salem, 62659.
217/632-7953. 180 sites. Showers, snack bar, store, swimming. Near Petersburg.
Lake Jacksonville. South of Jacksonville, 63650. 217/245-6903
or 245-8895. 300 sites. Showers, swimming, store, snack
bar.
Lake Springfield KOA. R R #2. Rochester, 62563. 217/637-
7002. 180 sites. Showers, swimming, store, snack bar.

Sangchris Lake State Park. R R #1, Rochester, 62563. 217/637-9208. 120 sites. Hiking trails.

INFORMATION:
Springfield Chamber of Commerce, 3 West Old State, Capitol Plaza, Suite 1, 62701. 217/525-1173.
Petersburg Chamber of Commerce, Box 452, 62675. 217/632-3241.

LODGING:
Dunlap Motor Inn. 331 W. State St., 62650. 40 rooms. 217/245-7121.
Holiday Inn. U.S. 36-54 West. (1717 W. Morton) 62650. 217/245-9571.
Star Lite Motel. U.S. 36-54. (1910 W. Morton) 62650. 217/245-7184.

SPRINGFIELD:
Abraham Lincoln Motel. 2929 S. 6th St., 62703. 217/544-1701.
Over a dozen other motels in Springfield. Write Chamber of Commerce.

RESTAURANTS:
Village Pump in Jacksonville. 5-10 p.m. 217/243-9937. Closed Sunday, major holidays.
Blackhawk Village. Cafeteria. 11 a.m.-2p.m., 5-8:30 p.m., closed Monday, also first two weeks in July, last week in December.
Other food chains in Jacksonville, Springfield, St. Petersburg.

BIKE CARE:
C.A.R. in Jacksonville, 217/243-3425.
Springfield Cycle and Lock, in Springfield. 217/787-2312.
Village Bike Shop. West off of South Main Street, Jacksonville. 217/245-5527.

TRANSPORTATION:
Air service, train, and bus to Springfield. Air service to Jacksonville.

Jacksonville to New Salem Map

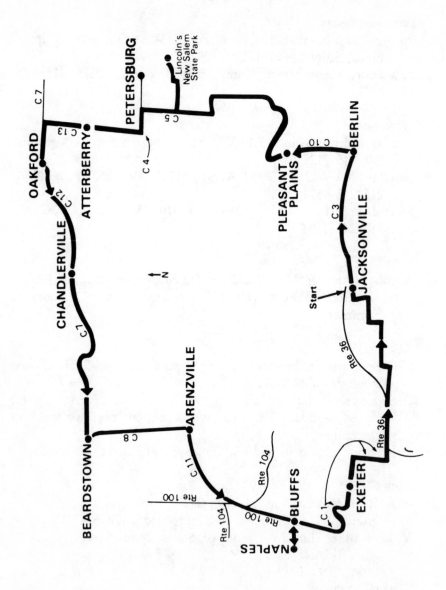

SHAWNEE NATIONAL FOREST TRIP

Southern Illinois, called "the other Illinois," by writer and philosopher Baker Brownwell, is a land of lush beauty and varied wildlife. Vastly different from the prairie that covers most of the state, this area is also known as "Little Egypt."

Also referred to as the "Illinois Ozarks," this part of the state has strong ties to the South. Cairo is further south than is Richmond, Va.

Magnolia, bald cypress, tupelo, canebrake, azaleas, and other Southern flora abound here. Cotton is cultivated, as are peach, apple, and pear orchards, and the people speak with the soft open-vowel pronunciation of Dixie.

This trip goes through the Shawnee National Forest, 240,000 acres of land wedged between the Mississippi and Ohio rivers. These foothills of the Ozark mountains are clothed by a massive blanket of trees, and cover nine Illinois counties. Profiles of stone, towering hills, secluded caves, bluffs, prehistoric stone forts, petroglyphs, waterfalls, lakes, and streams are part of the scenery.

This area was the first part of Illinois to be developed and was settled heavily by the French. The first capital of the state, Kaskaskia, stood north of Murphysboro, where your trip begins, until it was washed away by the Mississippi. All that remains now is a park commemorating its existence.

Wildlife is plentiful in the area. A native population of 20,000 wild turkeys live in the forest, and in fall and winter, 300,000 honking Canadian geese can be viewed at Crab Orchard Lake and in the marshlands of the Union Conservation Area along the Mississippi River. Enjoy the sight of eagles soaring above you, but be careful of the water moccasin, found in sluggish waters in the lowlands, and of the common wood rattler.

Bike through old river towns that speak of faded wealth and old lace. These towns prospered until the railroads branched out to move freight and took business from the river traffic. One community along the Ohio River, Old Shawnee-town, has attained some notoriety for refusing a loan in the early 1800s to an obscure village called Chicago. Shawnee-town bankers thought it a poor risk—the town was too far away ever to amount to anything.

Begin your trip in Murphysboro and proceed south from Harrisburg, entering the Illinois Ozarks, which reach heights of more than 1,000 feet above sea level. The heavily wooded slopes, slashed with deep ravines, change colors spectacularly with the seasons.

Pass Fountain Bluff, along the Mississippi River. Fountain Bluff is a six mile bluff jutting from the level floor plain and has many springs flowing from it.

Tower Rock is 60 feet high and an acre large and is the smallest National Park in America. Here take route 146 past the Union County Conservation Area, a wintering place for geese along the Mississippi bottomlands. Each year, a variety of hard grain and green foliage crops, such as corn, sunflower, wheat, and clover are cultivated and then left standing to provide food for wintering geese. This is a good area to capture the geese on film in the fall, but there are no overnight facilities in the immediate area so as not to disturb the waterfowl.

For information write:

Site Manager
Union County Conservation Area
RR 2
Jonesboro 62952
phone: 618/833-5175

Bike across the state to Cave In Rock on the Ohio River, 100 miles away. Cave In Rock is a 108-foot-deep cavern that was a holy place for Indians and a hiding place for river pirates who enjoyed its spectacular view of the Ohio River.

Throughout the Shawnee National Forest there are many modern, well-equipped campsites and dozens of hiking trails.

LOCATION:
Southern Illinois in Jackson, Union, Johnson, Pope, Hardin, Gallatin, Saline, and Williamson counties.

TERRAIN:
Hilly.

TRAVEL: Approximately 200 miles.

TIME:
2–4 days.

ROAD SURFACE:
Paved.

TYPE OF TRIP:
Tour or camp.

ROUTE:
Begin at Lake Murphysboro State Park in Jackson County. Take route 149 west to 3, south to 146 (Ware), east through Jonesboro and Golconda to 1, north to 13, west (through town of Crab Orchard) to Old Route 13, west to 149, west back to Murphysboro.

WHEN TO GO:
Spring through fall.

INFORMATION:
District Ranger, Murphysboro, Ill. 62966, for map of Shawnee National Forest.
Chamber of Commerce, Murphysboro, 62966.
Chamber of Commerce, Shawneetown, 62984.

CAMPING:
Lake Murphysboro State Park. RR 4. Murphysboro, 62966. 618/684-2867. 77 sites. Showers, store, snack bar.
Devil's Backbone Park, Box 11, Grand Tower, 62942. 618/565-2252. 40 sites.
Shady Lane Park, Rt 1, Grand Tower, 62942. 25 sites. Showers.
Shawnee Bluff Natural Theatre. Rt 127, Box 956, Murphysboro, 62966. 618/684-6821 or 684-4421. 62 sites.

Tower Rock, Shawnee National Forest, Elizabethtown, 62931. 618/287-2201. 35 sites.

Grapevine Trail. Shawnee National Forest near McClure. U.S. Forest Service, Jonesboro, 62952. 618/833-8576. 10 sites.

Hamilton County Conservation Area, Dolan Lake, RR 4, McLeansboro, 62859. 618/733-4340. 61 sites.

Camp Cadiz. Shawnee National Forest, Elizabethtown, 62931. 618/287-2201. 4 sites.

Steamboat Hill-Ohio River Recreation Area, Shawnee National Forest, U.S. Forest Service, Vienna, 62995. 618/658-2111. 17 sites.

Crab Orchard Recreation Area, RR 2, Carbondale, 62901. 618/985-6913. 300 sites. Showers, store, snack bar, swimming.

Devil's Kitchen Boat Dock, RFD 3, Carbondale, 62958. 618/457-5004. 48 sites. Showers, store, snack bar, swimming.

LODGING:

Holiday Inn of Carbondale, 800 E. Main, 62901. 618/457-2151.

Marion Courts, 110 S. Court St (State 37), Marion. 618/993-8131.

Murphysboro Motel, 100 N. 2nd St, 62965. 80 rooms. 618/687-2345.

RESTAURANTS:

Cave In Rock. On Ohio River at end of State 1. 618/289-3999. Fast food places in Carbondale, Marion and other towns.

BIKE CARE:

Carbondale Cycle Shop. 618/549-6863.

TRANSPORTATION:

Bus to Carbondale and Harrisburg. Train to Carbondale. Air service to Carbondale, Murphysboro.

Map of Shawnee National Forest Bike Trip

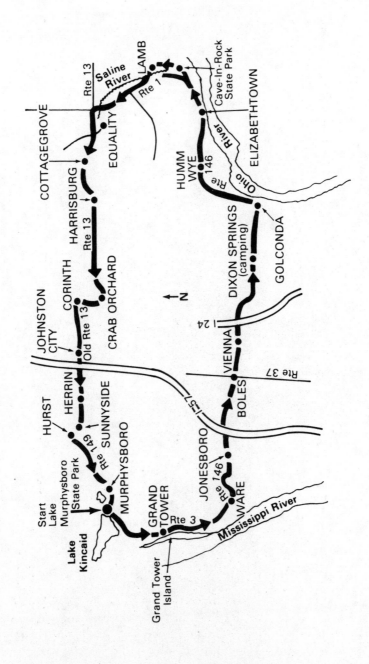

6

Indiana: Introduction and Trails

State Capital: Indianapolis
State Flower: Peony
State Tree: Tulip Tree
State Bird: Cardinal
State Nickname: "Hoosier State"

Hoosiers tell a story about the summer it was so hot, the corn popped in the fields. Don't let this tale discourage you from biking here, however, for it says more about the wry humor of these robust people than it does about Indiana's weather.

Most Indianians are descendants of pioneer stock, with traditions that combine Southern hospitality and Yankee shrewdness. They have an avid interest in local politics, and have formed many infamous organizations throughout the years to propagate their beliefs, such as the Know Nothing

Rural Indiana is loaded with picturesque places to park your bike and enjoy the serenity.

Party, the Mugwumps, the Klu Klux Klan and, more recently, the John Birch Society.

Fiercely independent, many of them chop their own wood, scorn government programs, and won't accept social security because, when it comes to aid, they'd rather do it themselves.

Heavy metal campgrounds full of RV's with all the riggings are found throughout the state and yet, Hoosiers are open and neighborly toward bikers, if you aren't condescending or frivolous. Talking with them can be an experience, for many will chat for hours, even to recounting how their great-grandfather came to the state decades ago.

Except for Northwest Indiana, near Gary, industry is woven into the fabric of farmland and villages. Small towns abound in this state, and the villages have wonderfully creative names such as Bean Blossom, Zulu, Popcorn, Gnaw Bone, Carp, Young America, Art, Friendship, and Farmer's Retreat.

Their inhabitants typify the rugged individuals who settled this country—inventive, hard working, and proud of their heritage and land. This pride in their state is well-justified. About two-thirds of Indiana is level, or gently rolling hills, and a smaller portion in the south is hilly, with the highest point being in Randolph County near the eastern border, at 1,285 feet.

The state is divided into three regions—the northern lake country, a lovely, pastoral area with many small, clear lakes nestled in low hills, and gigantic sand dunes lining lake Michigan; the central agricultural plain; and the more varied southern section, with tumbled hills, narrow valleys, lowlands, and tiny hamlets.

The Indiana Dunes National Lakeshore on Lake Michigan is an interesting area of great shifting sand dunes. "The Calumet Trail," a bikeway that is part of the Hoosier State Bikeway System, follows lake Michigan in the Dunes State Park and the Indiana Dunes National Lakeshore.

Other unusual features of the state are the Muscatatuck

National Wildlife Refuge, Pokagon State Park, where arrow-heads and other Indian relics can be found, Brown County State Park, the largest Indiana state park, which offers remarkable autumn colors, and the 156,000-acre Hoosier National Forest. Turkey Run and Shades state parks are noted for the virgin forests that still stand within them. For information and maps on these areas write:

> Department of Natural Resources
> Division of State Parks
> 616 State Office Building
> Indianapolis 46204

Marengo, in Southern Indiana, is a "fairyland" of caverns, and Wyandotte Cave is one of the world's largest caves. Near Orangeville, the Lost River, which flows underground for miles, finally surfaces. Such sights can be interesting side trips for the biker who travels these beautiful hills and valleys. One advantage of visiting caves is that even if the temperature outside is 80 degrees, inside the cave you'll stay a cool 58 degrees.

The Hoosier Bikeway System, when completed, will have hundreds of miles of scenic bike routes which will connect cities and recreation areas throughout the state. Routes will use lightly traveled, paved country roads that pass through quiet towns, and are away from the mainstream of auto and truck traffic. The Hoosier System brochures have some nice features, such as a profile map of the routes, which shows the approximate changes in elevation, and distances between major check points, as well as a map of the area.

In addition to the Calumet Trail mentioned above, the Whitewater Valley Route, from Batesville through Whitewater State Park and on to Richmond, is also a completed section of the Bikeway.

For information and maps of the 3 completed trails of the Hoosier Bikeway system, write:

State of Indiana
Department of Natural Resources
Division of Outdoor Recreation
612 State Office Building
Indianapolis 46204

If you bike in Parke County, you'll see many picturesque covered bridges, built in the 1800s, that are rustic and scenic reminders of our past. The protected structures of the bridges made them superior to the wood trestle bridges of the time, and were useful protection during storms, as well as secluded spots for courting. Hence their nickname, "kissing bridges." A vigorous effort to save the bridges resulted in 38 out of the 50 in the state being preserved.

The covered bridges are spectacular when framed by fall colors. A two week annual Covered Bridge Festival has been held each autumn since 1957, with narrated bus tours, chickens barbecued by the thousands on open spits, farmer's markets, and other festivities. These activities are primarily held in Parke County, Shades and Turkey Run state parks. The festival is listed as one of the top 10 tourist attractions in the United States by the U.S. Department of Interior. If you go in fall you'll see many colors, but you'll have to deal with heavy traffic, both from vehicles and other bikers.

You might consider biking the area in spring or summer, when the roads are not as busy, especially if youngsters are biking with you.

While in Parke County, stop at Billie Creek Village, one mile east of Rockville on U.S. 36. You can stroll through a village of a bygone era, pet and feed farm animals, and watch soap, candles, and brooms being made.

For tour information on seven bike routes in the county, most of them approximately 40 miles long that circle the covered bridges, write:

Covered Bridge Bicycle Tours
Box 165

Rockville, Indiana 47872
812/569-5226

In June, the town of Bean Blossom hosts an annual Blue-grass Music Festival, one of the best events of its kind.

The Parke County Maple Fair has been celebrated every May since 1964, while the city of Fort Wayne sponsors a Fine Arts Festival. The Indiana State Division of Tourism has excellent free calendars of these festivals, sports, and other events for the year. They will also send you a booklet listing camping areas in the state, and hotels and motels listed by town, if you write to:

State of Indiana
Division of Tourism
Room 336
State House
Indianapolis 46204

You can bike through the University of Indiana campus in Bloomington and enjoy this lovely area, as well as get a taste of campus life, or pedal in Spencer County, east of Evansville, where Abraham Lincoln spent the years between the ages of 14 and 21. A trip in this chapter covers this locale.

For tour guides and maps of interesting bike routes in Anderson, Bloomington, Columbus, Elkhart, Evansville, Fort Wayne, Hobart, Indianapolis, Kokomo, Ligonier, Mario, New Palestine, and Noblesville, write:

Department of Commerce
Room 336
State House
Indianapolis 46204

Wherever you go in this state, you'll find small towns, forests, and friendly people who are sentimental about their idyllic surroundings. After a bike trip in Indiana, chances are you'll feel the same way.

INDIANA BIKE RULES

In Indiana, bikers must use the right lane in traffic and obey all vehicle traffic regulations. Don't ride more than two abreast, except on paths set aside for the exclusive use of bikers. Bikers must have a bell or other audible device that can be heard from 100 feet away, but no sirens or whistles are allowed on bikes. After dusk and before dawn you must have a light which can be seen from 500 feet away, and a red rear reflector.

KOSCIUSKO COUNTY LAKE COUNTRY*

William Herschel's nostalgic poem, "Ain't God Good to Indiana," could be about almost any part of the state, but you'll understand his fondness for the green pastures, rippling waters, and sunshine on clover as you bike this civilized trip in resort country. On this trip you pedal into a country of wildflowers, meadows and woodlands. You have light traffic, and lots of lakes and lovely countryside.

Just north of this area, the town of Elkhart is the band instrument capital of the world. The Howe Military Academy is nearby, as is Pokagon State Park, Chain o' Lakes State Park, and the vacation resort areas.

Twenty-five miles southeast of the trip, Fort Wayne offers summer theatre, art shows, and many good restaurants.

Several herds of deer roam this part of the state, and if you're alert, you may see them browsing in the forests and fields.

There are many fast food restaurants as well as snack shops such as ice cream parlors. You'll start this trip in Atwood, about six miles from Warsaw, and ride around the lakes and through farm country in the area.

The trip will go around 25 of the 100 lakes in Kosciusko County. You can take a 25-mile, 50-mile, or 100-mile tour (see map). Surrounding the lakes are small grocery stores, quiet

---

*Route courtesy of Gaylord Johnston, Warsaw Area Wheeler's Bike Club.

resorts, and many camping areas. Stop at fruit stands along the way, or attend nearby events such as chicken barbecues in summer, sailboat races, and county fairs. At Oswego, 10 miles from Warsaw, you can browse through the county historical museum.

LOCATION:
Northern Indiana, about 100 miles east and south of Chicago, in Kosciusko County.

TERRAIN:
Flat to rolling farmland.

TRAVEL:
25, 50, or 100 miles.

TIME:
One or two days.

ROAD SURFACE:
Paved; light traffic.

TYPE OF TRIP:
Day, tour, or camp.

ROUTE:
Begin in Atwood. Take 650W south to 100N, east across tracks to 350W, north to 300N, east to 300W, north to 400N, east to Monoquet to SR15, north to Levi Lee Road, east and north to 100E, south to 450N, east to 175E, south to 150E, south to 300N, east to 175E, south to 175N, east to 300E, north around lake to Stoneburner Road, north to 450, west to 300E, north (either cut over on 300E north to 700N west on the 35 mile loop home; or continue on) to Armstrong Road around lake to 475E, south to 400N, southeast to McKenna Road, east to 400N, east (either cut over on 850E north—see map—for 60 mile loop, or continue on) to 925E, north to 450N, east to SR5, north

to 1100W, south to 350S, east to 450W, north to SR109 to U.S. 33, northwest to 100S, west to Knapp Lake Road, west to 975W, north to 100N, west to 1150W, north to 200N, west to Koher Road around lake to Papakeechie Road, around lake to Eli Lilly Road to Warner to 625E, into Syracuse to Syracuse-Webster Road, south to 500E, south to 650N, west to Country Club, northwest to 750N, west to 300E, south to 700N, west through Leesburg to 400W, south to 600N, west to 600W, south to 400N, west to 700W, south into Atwood.

WHEN TO GO:
Spring through fall.

CAMPING:
Lake Tippecanoe. 9 miles northeast of Warsaw on CR 700N. Store. April 15–October 15. Leesburg, 46538. 219/453-3671.

Lozier's Campground. Warsaw. 2 miles east on "old" U.S. 30. North on CR 300E. Showers. May 15–October 15. Route 6, Warsaw, 46580. 219/267-3215.

Monoquet Meadows. Warsaw. 4 miles north on SR 15. 1 mile west on CR 500N. May–November 1. Laundry, showers, store, food service. Route 7, Warsaw, 46580.

Pike Lake Campground. Warsaw. 4 blocks east of SR 15 on Arthur Street. April 15–October 1. City of Warsaw Park Department. 46580. 219/269-1439.

Tri-County Fish and Wildlife Area. Warsaw. 20 miles north on CR 900N. Box 358, Syracuse, 46567. 219/834-4461.

INFORMATION:
Kosciusko County Sheriff's Department, 219/267-5667.
Kosciusko Community Hospital, 219/267-3200.
Chamber of Commerce, 124 W Market St, Warsaw, 46580. 219/267-6311.

LODGING:
Warsaw Holiday Inn, 219/269-2323.

Kosciusko Lake Country Trail Map

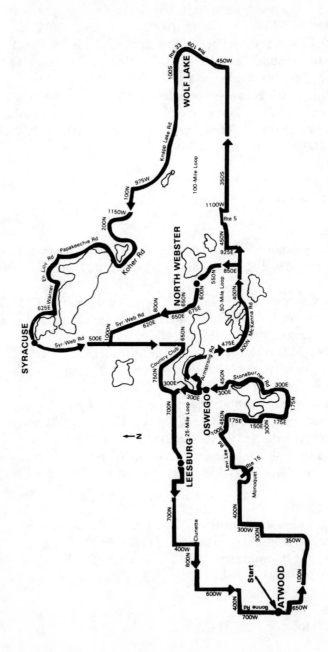

RESTAURANTS:
Several fast food chains along the route. Contact the Chamber
of Commerce.

BIKE CARE:
Freewheelin' Bicycles, 211 West Center, Warsaw. 219/267-
3767.

TRANSPORTATION:
Bus to Warsaw. Air service to South Bend. Train to Fort
Wayne.

AMISHLAND AND LAKE COUNTRY*

Quaint, horse-drawn buggies in the Amish settlements, rural
countryside, and sparkling blue lakes are just part of the
charm of this easy ride in northern Indiana and the southern
lakes section of Michigan.

Start at the town of Howe, Indiana, about twenty miles
from the Ohio border and not far from I-90. The first day's
trip winds through Amish farm country in Indiana. Ride past
colorful gardens in tiny early American towns, and share the
road with clip-clopping horses pulling Amish carriages. The
roads are lightly traveled and quiet; many are partly shaded.

Descendants of the Swiss Anabaptists, the Amish follow an
early Christianity, and live primarily in Pennsylvania, Ohio,
and Indiana. Church services are in German, and their
communities are very religious and patriarchal. Language,
customs, and dress are dictated by community rules, and they
have no phones, electricity, tractors, musical instruments, or
education beyond elementary school. Because they resist
change, their life-style is very close to what it was in the
1600s.

Since their religion forbids photographs, they will be highly
offended if you try to take pictures of them. However, you

---

*Route courtesy of Marv Scher, Michiana Bicycle Association in Granger,
Indiana.

can film their gardens, horses and buggies, and shops. Behind the courthouse in LaGrange, rows of buggies usually stand on the brick street and make good subjects for photography.

The Howe Military School, founded in 1833, has an old world style chapel and a beautiful campus.

At Hobbs Marsh, a swamp north of LaGrange, well-preserved bones and a mastodon skull have been found.

In the unspoiled town of Topeka, Amish tradesmen work at their crafts of blacksmithing, carriage making, and horseshoeing, in a style reminiscent of the 19th century. Saturday morning, the streets are lined with horses and carriages.

In Shipshewana, the auction barn draws many Amish settlers, who do their shopping. Public restrooms, water, and food are available here.

On the second day, head north into Michigan. The excellent roads, very light traffic, easy, rolling hills, lakes, and forests make Cass County, Michigan, a biker's dream.

There are stores and restrooms at Corey Lake, Jones, Zimmeville, Bristol, and Eby's Pines.

Start this trip 17 miles due west of Saturday's ride, at Bonneyville Mill Park. Before you begin, visit the grist mill at the park, built in 1832, which has an unusual horizontal water wheel. Amish craftsmen helped preserve many authentic features of the mill during its reconstruction.

In a cemetery just east of the mill, on county road 8, is the grave of William Tufts, who participated in the Boston Tea Party, was a revolutionary soldier, and lived eventfully until the age of 108.

North of Constantine you enter hill and lake country, and ride past more than 14 lakes. You also see the St. Joseph River both early and late in the ride.

Jones was restored to resemble a turn-of-the-century American town, but has returned to being a ghost town. Only the saloon is open.

In Bristol, visit the Rush Memorial Historical Museum, which is housed in an old school building and contains clothing and tools of the pioneers who settled Elkhart County.

There is no fee. Bristol also has an old fashioned soda fountain east of the traffic light.

LOCATION:
Northeast Indiana in Elkhart and LaGrange counties. Southern Michigan in St. Joseph and Cass counties.

TERRAIN:
Flat to lightly rolling hills.

TRAVEL:
100 miles.

TIME:
2 days.

ROAD SURFACE:
Paved, light traffic.

TYPE OF TRIP:
Tour or camp.

ROUTE:
First day. Begin in Howe. Take 600N east to 100E, south to SR 9, south through LaGrange to Hawpatch Road, southwest to 200W, south to 550S, west to 300W, south to 700S, west (Topeka) to 600W, north through Emma to U.S. 20, north to 100N, east to 25N, east to 250W, north to 200N, west to SR 5, north through Shipshewana to 250N, east to 275N, east to 300N, east and north to 400W, north to 400N, east to 100W, north to 600N, east into Howe.

Second day. Begin at Bonneyville Mill. Take CR 131 north to CR 8, east to CR 35, north to Barker, east to CR 116, north to Riverside Drive, north and east into Constantine to U.S. 131, northwest to Prairie, northwest to Youngs, northwest to M60, east to Lake Jones, north to South Corry Lake, west to Born, west to M40, south through

Jones to Bair Lake, east to M40, south to Harvey St. West, south around Birch Lake to Birch Road, south to U.S. 12, east to Sunset Blvd, south into Indiana. CR 2 east to CR 25, southwest into Bristol. CR 8 east to CR 131 to Bonneville Mill.

WHEN TO GO:
Spring through fall.

CAMPING:
Howe: Riverside Camp. 5 miles west of 120, then 1/3 mile north on CR 450W. 60 sites. Showers. May 1–November 1.
Twin Mills Resort. 2 miles W on 120. 150 sites. Showers, store.
LaGrange: Pigeon River State Fish and Game Area. 7 miles east on 201. 3 miles north on 3. ½ mile east on CR 300N. 42 sites.
Elkhart, Indiana: Eby's Pines. 10 miles north of Goshen on 15. 3 miles east on 120. May 1–November 1.
Union, Michigan: Hollywood Shores Resort. 1 mile east on 12. 1½ miles south on Baldwin-Prairie Rd. 1 mile east on Wayne St. 42 sites. May 1–October 1.
Willow Shores Campers Resort. 1 mile east on 12. 120 sites. Showers, laundry, store.

INFORMATION:
Chamber of Commerce, Box 428, Elkhart, Ind. 46514. 219/293-1531.
LaGrange Chamber of Commerce, Box 95, LaGrange, Ind. 46761. 219/463-2443.
LaGrange, Ind., County Police, 219/463-3111. Ambulance, 219/463-7118.
Elkhart, Ind., County Police, 219/533-8644. Ambulance, 219/293-9720.
Cass County, Mich., police, 616/663-5225.
St. Joseph County, Mich., police, 616/467-9045.
Three Rivers, Mich., ambulance, 616/278-2055.

Amishland and Lake Country Maps

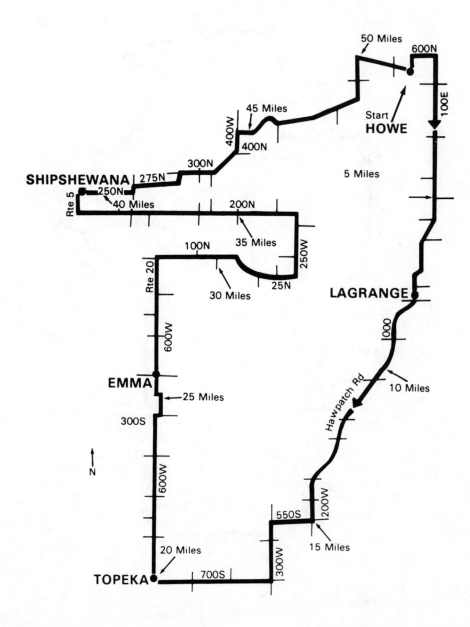

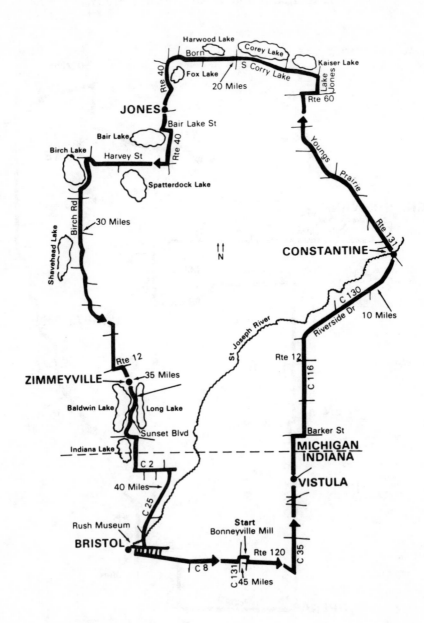

LODGING:

Elkhart Indiana: Holiday Inn. 2725 Cassopolis. Pool. 219/264-7502.

Traveler's Inn. 220 W. Jackson Boulevard (U.S. 30). 219/524-1493.

Grace Motel. 2244 W. Lexington (U.S. 20). 219/294-2833.

RESTAURANTS:

Minelli's Steak House in Elkhart, Indiana. Harrison and 6th Sts. 219/522-1226.

Pizza Hut. 4 miles north of Howe on Highway 9.

McDonald's fast food and other places in towns along the route.

BIKE CARE:

Howe: Lincoln Avenue Schwinn Cyclery. 219/533-7425.

Angola (about 25 miles east and south of Howe): The Western Auto Association Store. 219/665-5662.

TRANSPORTATION:

Air service to South Bend, Indiana. Bus to LaGrange, Indiana, and Sturgis, Michigan (5 miles due north of Howe). Train to Elkhart, Indiana.

BLOOMINGTON'S HILLY HUNDRED*

Every fall, the Central Indiana Bicycle Association (CIBA) hosts a ride along this route, on which over a thousand bicyclists from all over the country participate. It is one of the outstanding bicycle events in the nation, and whether you ride, or just watch, it is thrilling to see close to 100 lines of 15 riders each, dressed in brightly colored clothing, ease out of the high school parking lot in Bloomington, and establish their own pace as they pedal down the streets.

One rolling hill after another along the route prompted a

---

*Route courtesy of Judi and Ross Faris, Central Indiana Bicycle Association, Indianapolis, Indiana.

biker to mourn recently, "Wouldn't you know, the only flat areas around here are the lakes!"

The ride is strenuous, but not impossible. Among those who conquered the 100 miles of hills in Brown and Monroe counties in 1977 were a 6-year-old girl, a 7-year-old boy, a 62-year-old woman and a 73-year-old man.

You don't have to ride with the CIBA, however, to enjoy the steep climbs, breezy descents, and cool forests of this trip in the glacier-formed foothills of the Appalachian mountains.

And the roads do obey the law of physics: everything that goes up must come down. There are many long, downhill swoops that give you a good boost up the next hill before you get down to real pedaling up the top portion of the rise.

The challenge and grandeur of the tour will renew your spirit and confidence. There are no towns or restaurants on the first day's route, however, so be sure to bring plenty of food, water, and energy snacks to renew your physical strength. You ride through a gorgeous state forest with absolutely no commercial establishments or houses.

The second day's ride is slightly easier, and goes through the charming old town of Nashville, Indiana. Tour shops such as the Brown County Art Gallery, Pewter Palace, Brown County Peddler (antiques), and Grasshopper Flats (handcrafted items).

You'll also pass the Bean Blossom Fruit Stand, where you can get something to eat.

The roads are all hard surfaced, with a few miles of rough road.

Remember that Bloomington is a college town, with the lovely campus of Indiana University located in the city. It has good places to eat, motels, and lots of museums, but can be very crowded if you go in the fall on a football weekend. You may have trouble getting lodging on such days.

This trip is not far from scenic Brown County State Park.

LOCATION:
Southern Indiana, Monroe and Brown counties.

TERRAIN:
Hilly.

TRAVEL:
100 miles.

TIME:
2 days.

ROAD SURFACE:
Paved, light traffic.

TYPE OF TRIP:
Tour or camp.

ROUTE:
First day. Start in Bloomington. Take Kinser Pike north to
Bottom Road, north to Maple Grove Road, west (Bad
Bridge Town) and north to Mt. Tabor, north to
Brighton, northeast to North Road, north to Parragon
Road, east across the 4-lane route 37 to Old-old 37, east
to Main Forest Road, east to Bean Blossom Road, south
around Bean Blossom Lake to Anderson Road, south and
west to Old-old 37, south back into Bloomington.
Second Day. Begin in Bloomington. Take Bethel Lane east to
SR 45, east (through Unionville) to Helmsburg Road,
south to Greasy Creek Road, north (Bean Blossom Fruit
Mkt) to SR 45, west to South Shore Road, west to
Robinson Road, west to the town of Dolan. Take Old-old
37 south to Bloomington.

WHEN TO GO:
Spring through fall.

CAMPING:
Nashville, Indiana: Brown County State Park. 3 miles south
on 135. 127 sites. Showers, store, pool.

RVP KOA. Brown County. 2½ miles east on 46. 110 sites. Showers, laundry, store, pool. April 1–November 1.

Walden Ridge Campgrounds. 7 miles east on 46. 50 sites.

Yellowwood State Forest. 7 miles west on 46. 50 sites.

Monroe Reservoir State Recreation Area. 10 miles southeast of Bloomington via 46 and 446. 355 sites. Showers, store, lake swimming. Easter–October 15.

Leisure Land Campgrounds. Bloomington. 4 miles south on New Highway 37, 1½ mile east on Smithville Road, then 1½ mile south on Fairfax. 115 sites. Showers. May 1–October 1.

INFORMATION:

Bloomington Chamber of Commerce, 220 S. Walnut, Box 1302, 47401. 812/336-6381.

Nashville Chamber of Commerce, Box 164, Indiana 47448. 812/988-4920.

LODGING:

Holiday Inn, 2 miles north of New 37, Bloomington, 812/332-9453.

Stony Crest, 1300 N. Walnut, Bloomington, 812/332-9491.

Abe Martin Lodge, in Brown County State Park. Box 25, Nashville, 812/988-4418.

Brown County Inn, at Indiana 46 and 135. Nashville, 812/988-2291.

RESTAURANTS:

Grove's Restaurant, Indiana University campus, Bloomington.

Nick's English Pub (pizza and sandwiches), Indiana University campus, Bloomington.

The Fireside, 205 N. College, Bloomington, 812/332-2141.

Tudor Room, Indiana University campus, Bloomington, 812/337-1620.

Colonial Room and Granny's Pantry, Nashville, 812/988-7900.

The Ordinary, Nashville, 812/988-6166.

Dairy Queen/Brazier, Jct 46 and 135, Nashville, 812/988-7100.

Two Maps of Bloomington's Hilly Hundred

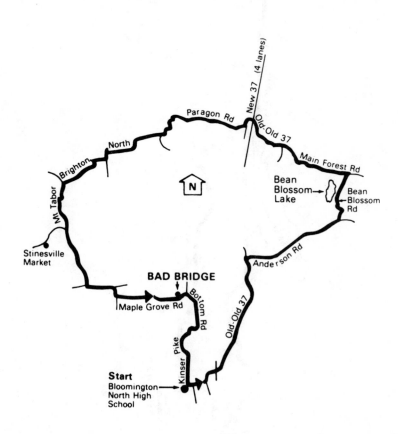

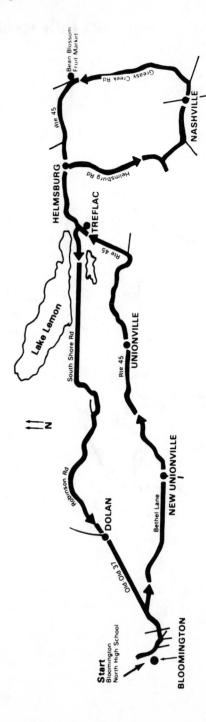

BIKE CARE:
Bicycle Doctor, Bloomington, 812/825-5050.
Bloomington Cyclery, 812/336-0241.
Bike Rack, Bloomington, 812/339-8791.

TRANSPORTATION:
Air service, bus, and trains to Bloomington.

HILLS AND HISTORY IN SOUTHERN INDIANA*

Rolling country backroads with almost no traffic on them are the rule on this trip. At times you may not see a car in half an hour. What you will see and experience is a lot of gently rolling hills, with a couple of good climbs coming into French Lick from the town of Vincennes.

There is a remarkable amount of history in these hills. The town of Vincennes was at one time the most important city in the Midwest, and speculators bought Chicago land here for 25 cents an acre.

St. Meinrad Archabbey, built in 1852, was constructed of native stone by the Benedictine Fathers. The abbey is famous for its choirs and altars, and church services are held exactly as they have been for the last thousand years in Switzerland.

Figure at least six days for this trip, which takes in the historic towns of New Harmony, Vincennes, French Lick, St. Meinrad, the town of Santa Claus, Lincoln's boyhood home, and Angel Mounds in Evansville.

These backroads were carefully selected by Edgar Whitcomb, a former governor of Indiana who is an ardent cyclist. He toured this area with the League of American Wheelmen in the mid-70s.

Some highlights on this gorgeous trip that takes you miles from civilization and then back into it are St. Meinrad, where lodging is very reasonable and food is superb, and French Lick, where you begin.

---

*Route courtesy of Phyllis Harmon, League of American Wheelmen, Palatine, Illinois.

In Santa Claus, you'll find the jolly man in the red suit, as well as his helpers, elves, favorite animal characters, and live deer. Send a postcard from this enchanting land, for the Santa Claus Post Office, originally established in 1856, has a world famous postmark.

Bike on to Gentryville and Lincoln's boyhood home, only five miles west of Santa Claus Land, then through Folsomville and into Boonville, named after Daniel Boone. The country along this trip is noted for its natural beauty, and scenic drives are framed by lush hardwood forests.

If you bike in April, you can participate in the Dogwood Festival in Perry County. Tell City's Schweizer Fest is held in August, and a Fall Festival is celebrated in October.

You ride through the Lincoln Hills, part of the Hoosier National Forest, which has over 56,000 acres in Perry County and contains a wild turkey preserve.

The prevailing winds here are from the South, and the weather is mild. In autumn the hills are painted with color, and clear, cool days often last into December.

In the busy city of Evansville visit the Angel Mounds, the site of a large prehistoric Indian town which flourished on the banks of the Ohio River from 1300 to 1500 A.D. The Angel Mounds Memorial is at 8215 Pollack Avenue, seven miles east of downtown Evansville, four blocks south of State Road 662. For information write: Division of Museums and Memorials, Department of Natural Resources, 202 N. Alabama St., Indianapolis, Ind. 46204. Phone 317/633-4948.

Evansville has a July 4th Freedom Festival, the Ohio River Arts Festival, and many bierstubes, flea markets, art fairs, and auctions. If you have time, take a walking tour of Old Evansville, which begins at the museum.

In New Harmony, 30 miles west of Evansville, stop in the Visitor Information center and ask about a self-guided walking tour of the town. It was a nationally known site of two experimental communes in the early 1800s, and the birthplace of the Smithsonian Institution.

The town of Vincennes is on the Lincoln Heritage Trail, and offers a tourist train that is well worth taking. The tram winds through the historic areas of Vincennes and gives information on different decades of the town's past. Red Skelton's home, with a Red Skelton Bridge, is in Vincennes.

The ride between Vincennes and French Lick is 70 miles. You can do it in one day if you are in good shape, but you'll be working at it, as this part of the trip has steep hills.

Also on this trip you pass a scenic river overlook at Cannelton, where you can see the locks and dam, the quaint river town of Newburgh, and the "Point of Beginning" where the Northwest Territory Survey started, as well as other historical memorials.

LOCATION:
Southern Indiana, in 11 counties: Posey, Vanderburg, Warrick, Spencer, Perry, Crawford, Orange, Martin, Daviess, Knox, Gibson, and Pike.

TERRAIN:
Hilly.

TRAVEL:
250 miles.

TIME:
6 days.

ROAD SURFACE:
Paved.

TYPE OF TRIP:
Tour or camp.

ROUTE:
Begin in French Lick. Take 145 south to 64, west (Birds Eye) to 145, south to 460, west (St. Meinrad) to 62, west to 161, west and south (Lincoln's boyhood home) to 161, south and west (Boonville. Stay overnight here.) to 61, south (to Yankeetown) to 662, west (Angel Mounds) to

Evansville. Ride carefully through city traffic to N (to Darmstadt and Haubstadt) to 68, west to New Harmony. Retrace 68 east to Poseyville to 165, north to (Johnson) 65, north to 64, east (Princeton) to 65, north to 56, east (Petersburg) to 61, north (Vincennes. Stay overnight here). Retrace 61, south (Monroe city) to 241, northeast to 150, east (Washington) to 257, south to 231, north to 150, southeast to 145, south to French Lick.

WHEN TO GO:
Spring through fall.

CAMPING:
Harmonie State Park. East of New Harmony on 66. 812/682-4821.
U.S. Twin Lakes. 8 miles west on 62 from Evansville, then 1 mile south on Welborn Road. 50 sites. Pool. April 1–November 1.
In Wadesville, Country Living, 3 miles southeast on 460, then ½ mile north on St. Phillip Road. 40 sites.
Dougan's Overnight. 3 miles east on 460. 2 miles north on St. Phillips Road. 20 sites. Showers. April 1–November 30.
Lincoln State Park in Dale. 5 miles south on 231. 350 sites. Showers, store, lake swimming.
Kimmel Park in Vincennes. 2 miles northeast via Second and Portland streets. 250 sites. Showers. April 1–October 1.
KOA in Vincennes. 2 miles north on 41 at jct 67. 50 sites. Showers, laundry, store.
George Rogers Clark National Historical Park, 401 S. Second St., Vincennes, 47591. 812/882-1776.

INFORMATION:
Vincennes Chamber of Commerce, 417 Burreon St., 47591, 812/882-6440.
Evansville Chamber of Commerce, 329 Main St., 47708, 812/425-8147.
French Lick Chamber of Commerce, Box 347, 47432. 812/936-4704.

Hills and History in Southern Indiana Map

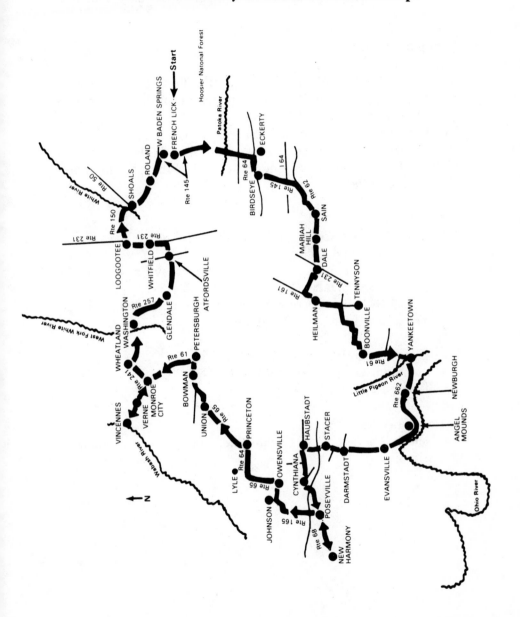

Lincoln Hills Tourist Association, P.O. Box 8, Cannelton, 47520.

LODGING: 21 motels in Evansville.

Holiday Inn, Evansville. 812/425-1092.

Jackson House, 20 Walnut St., Evansville. Pool. 812/423-7816.

Towne Motel, 15 NW Riverside Drive, Evansville. Overlooks Ohio River. Pool. 812/423-8071.

Lanes, State 56 in French Lick. 812/936-9919.

Stone's, 460 in Dale (near Santa Claus). 812/937-4448.

Holiday Inn in Vincennes, one motel in Newburgh, one motel in Boonville.

RESTAURANTS:

Joe Larvo's Three Coins in Evansville, 711 First Avenue, 11 a.m. to midnight, closed Sunday, holidays.

F's Steak House. 125 S.E. Fourth Street, Evansville. 11 a.m.–11 p.m., closed Sunday, holidays. 812/422-4189.

Marones, 101 North Second Street, Vincennes. 11 a.m. to 10 p.m., closed Sunday. 812/882-0460.

BIKE CARE: Seven bike shops in Evansville.

Art's Schwinn Gallery, Evansville, 812/479-8021.

Handlebar, Evansville, 812/476-0881.

TRANSPORTATION:

Air service and bus to Evansville. Train to Carbondale, Illinois.

7

Iowa: Introduction and Trails

State Capital: Des Moines
State Flower: Wild Rose
State Tree: Oak
State Bird: Eastern Goldfinch
State Nickname: "Hawkeye State"

Iowa is the New England of the Midwest; tidy towns with tall church spires and picket fences nestle on low hills. The state used to be a well-guarded secret of corn-fed farmers in bib overalls, who believed in the work ethic—and a place other people drove through on their way to someplace else. But as pollution, overcrowding, and crime become major concerns in the nation, Iowa is being discovered.

It has sunny fields, no crowds or traffic jams, strict anti-pollution laws, and one of the lowest serious crime rates in America. It is a place to grow. Its farms are prosperous; its people, genuine and friendly.

A typical Iowa roadside rest—next to one of its famous cornfields—makes a great place for a lunch stop.

Named after Indians who roamed the flat or gently rolling prairieland that comprises most of the state, Iowa means "beautiful land." Almost 90 percent of the land is farmed, and it has perhaps the richest soil in the country.

The state has visual as well as economic beauty. Because it's such an amazing producer of food, its natural beauty is often overlooked. Steep hills, 100 to 300 feet high, rise in a strip 20 miles wide along the Missouri River on the western border. Other rivers in the western part of the state are swiftly flowing, and rise quickly during heavy rainstorms.

In the north, small lakes left behind by glaciers have become the centers of resort areas. The northeast corner of the state, along the Mississippi River, is the most rugged part, with breathtaking panoramas of river and field. The majority of industries are located east of the Des Moines River.

Keokuk, at the southernmost point in the state, has the lowest elevation, 477 feet above sea level. From there, the land rises north and west, to the highest point of 1,670 feet at the state's northern border.

Iowa is a region of subtle contours, farm buildings sheltered by groves of trees, natural woodlands, irregular lines of bluffs, and knolly pastureland where large herds of stock feed. It is excellent biking country for families or friends. Small towns are seldom more than 10 miles apart, and yet traffic is light because there are few big cities. The secondary and county roads are, on the whole, well-surfaced.

Every year since 1972, several thousand riders participate in a bikeathon sponsored by the *Des Moines Register and Tribune* newspaper. Riders begin the week-long journey by first dunking their wheels in the Missouri River on the western border, then ride to the Mississippi River, where they cool their sizzling wheels once again. The route is changed each year and is held in either the month of July or August.

The bike trip, called RAGBRAI (for *Register's* Annual Great Bike Ride Across Iowa), was first taken by two newspaper-men in 1972. By 1977, 4,000 bikers were coming along. Anyone can ride the RAGBRAI; but bikers under 17 years of age must have an adult sponsor with them. The ride is for seasoned bikers; in 1978 the trip from Sioux City to Clinton totaled 440 miles, and included a 97-mile day.

The *Des Moines Register* promotion department contracts small towns along the route in advance, and makes arrange-ments with chambers of commerce for overnight stays and makes sure adequate food is available for the bikers. Bikers must bring their own tents.

RAGBRAI has mushroomed such that thousands of bikers have to be turned away each year when they ask for registration forms. Those who do go are leaner, tanner, and healthier at the end of the week.

This event has all the flavor of a state festival, a time when small towns of 500 people give a grand welcome to the 4,000 bikers that invade their communities once a year.

For more information on RAGBRAI write:

Des Moines Register and Tribune
c/o RAGBRAI
P.O. Box 957
Des Moines, Iowa 50304
Phone: 515/284-8000

You don't have to travel with 3,999 other bikers to enjoy Iowa's warm summer nights, and fields woven into a checkerboard of soybeans, wheat, corn, and pastureland.

In spring and summer, bloodroot, lilies, wild asters, wild roses, and other wildflowers bloom along the road; in the fall, the countryside dazzles with the brilliant colors of oaks, elms, maples, and hickory trees.

Many cities in the state have bikepaths. The Cinder Path, a 13-mile trail that runs between Chariton and Derby on the roadbed of an abandoned Burlington Railroad line, is a smooth cinder surface with an even grade. For information on this and other city bikeways write:

Park and Recreation Department
East First and Des Moines Streets
Des Moines, Iowa 50309

Biking facilities in Davenport are also excellent. You can ride along the Mississippi in Dubuque and visit the 162-acre Eagle Point Park, with its high promontories, sunken gardens, and pavillions that offer stunning views of the river. You can also see an old shot tower, a cable car, visit nearby Dickeyville grotto, or take a two-hour riverboat excursion down the Mississippi. Visit the Five Flags Theatre, built in 1910, and the county jail which is an example of Egyptian Revival Architecture.

Colorful personalities fill Iowa's history—Lewis and Clark, Jesse James, Buffalo Bill, Bonnie and Clyde, Herbert Hoover, and Mark Twain. The state has a thriving cultural life, with 54 community playhouses, 17 symphony orchestras, and 28 art centers and galleries. For information on festivals, fairs and other events in Iowa, as well as camping information, write:

Travel Development Division
Iowa Development Commission
250 Jewett Building
Des Moines, Iowa 50309

For County maps of the state, write:

Iowa Department of Transportation
Map Division
Ames, Iowa 50010

Maps cost 20 cents each plus 3 percent sales tax for ½ inch scale, or 10 cents each plus 3 percent sales tax for ¼ inch scale.

Cutting through the state, U.S. highway 30 passes many points of interest, such as the Desoto National Wildlife Refuge on the floodplain of the Missouri River. This area is a migration stopover for 400,000 geese and a million ducks annually. The National Goose Calling Festival is held in the Missouri Valley each fall, and in the same area, the Harrison County Historical Village has nine reconstructed pioneer buildings.

William Cody, later known as Buffalo Bill, was born near the Mississippi River town of LeClaire. His boyhood home, restored to its original condition, is open to the public, as is the Buffalo Bill museum. You can hike the one-mile Buffalo Bill trail to other historical sites.

The most exotic breed of beef cattle can be seen in Coon Rapids. For information on these and other points of interest along route 30 write:

Iowa U.S. 30 Association
306 West Lincolnway
Jefferson, Iowa 50129

The Lacey-Keosauqua Park, a beautiful wooded area in the southeast tip of Iowa, is also worth seeing. Situated along the bluffs of the Des Moines River, it has miles of trails, ancient Indian mounds, a 30-acre lake and 350 campsites.

The river town of Burlington has Dixieland Jazz festivals that draw top musicians from all parts of the country, and a Riverboat Days celebration each June.

To receive an Iowa Travel and Accommodations Guide, write:

> Iowa Hotel, Motel, Motor-Inn Association
> 515 28th Street
> Des Moines, Iowa 50312

This state has festivals and celebrations to honor everything from old threshing machines to beer and schnitzel. See historic river villages, enjoy rodeos, listen to the slosh-slosh of a sternwheeler as you ride a paddleboat down the Mississippi River, see 40 machines in perfect working order in the Nickelodeon Museum near Clinton, or visit the University of Iowa campus in Iowa City.

Or stick to the road, and enjoy the clean air, unspoiled countryside, and friendship and hospitality of the people as you bike. Whatever trip you plan, you'll find that the good old days are still around in Iowa.

IOWA BIKE RULES

The motor vehicle code for this state says simply that a bicycle is entitled to reasonable use of a highway, but that bikers must ride with caution and prudence. Your best bet is to obey all traffic laws for vehicles, and as always, ride defensively.

AMANA COUNTRY

On this trip, about thirty miles southeast of Cedar Rapids, you bike past cheery, sunlit meadows into the seven villages of the Amana religious community. The horse-drawn carriages, old world dress, and customs of another age will charm both adult and children bikers alike.

Known as the Amana Colonies, these communities were founded in 1854 and incorporated into the Amana Society in 1932. The Society owns and operates farmland and such businesses as the woolen mill, furniture factory, meat shops, and bakery. All properties are held in common, and families live in society-owned houses. Religious life is the strong unifying factor in the communities, and church services are held 11 times a week. Church elders decide all matters of religion, business, and government, and community members work, dine, and pray together in each of the villages.

The first six villages were built a distance of about an hour apart by oxcart, and each was responsible for farming the land around it. Later, the village of Homestead was purchased, to give the Amanas access to the railroad.

The Amana name is familiar to many who enjoy home cured meats, home spun woolens, sturdy, handcrafted furniture, and fine wines. Be sure to eat in one of the superb family style restaurants, which feature fine German foods. These colony restaurants are so noted for their excellent foods that you practically have to inherit the right to eat in them on important religious holidays such as Easter.

In the town of Homestead visit a restored, furnished colonial house. A woolen mill and furniture factory offer free hourly tours Monday through Friday from 10 a.m. to 4 p.m. in summer. See the Community Kitchen of a century ago at Middle Amana from April 1 through November 1, 9 a.m.–5 p.m. The Museum of Amana History tells how members of the Mormon faith, primarily of German, Swiss, and French stock, detrained from Iowa City in 1856. The museum is set in spacious grounds among grape arbors and gardens.

Many members of the sect seek the simple life and resist change, rejecting modern conveniences. Bikers should look out for horse-drawn vehicles on surface shoulders of the highways. The annual "Oktoberfest" draws many visitors to the communities each fall.

An impromptu foot-cooling stop by a handy riverbank.

In Kalona, in Amishland, the Kalona Historical and Mennonite Historical Societies sponsor the Fall Festival, featuring spinning, quilting, fresh-baked goods, and homemade apple butter the last Friday and Saturday of September.

For further information on the Amana Colonies, write:

>   Amana Heritage Society
>   Amana, Iowa 52203

For information on the Kalona Fall Festival write:

>   Chamber of Commerce
>   Washington, Iowa

While in the area, stop by Iowa's first permanent Capitol Building, built in 1840 and still standing in Iowa City at the center of the University of Iowa campus, and see the restored house of Robert Lucas, first governor of Iowa.

In Mount Pleasant, south of Iowa City, the Midwest Old Settlers and Threshers Association stages an annual reunion on the five days before Labor Day. Hundreds of steam engines, locomotives, and cars are in operation. On the reunion grounds, the Old Settlers Village, a restored pioneer town, has arts and crafts, threshing machine demonstrations, and a steam railroad.

LOCATION:
Eastern Iowa in Washington County.

TERRAIN:
Level.

TRAVEL:
80 miles.

TIME:
2 days.

ROAD SURFACE:
Paved.

TYPE OF TRIP:
Day, tour, or camp.

ROUTE:
Start at Lake MacBride State Park. Take 382 east to W6E (county road), north 1 mile to F12, 18 miles to 149, south 2 miles to 22D, east into East Amana, then west in Middle, High, and West Amana. Return to High Amana and take F15 west to V66, south 15 miles to F46, east into Iowa City. Take 1 north to Solon and then 382 west to Lake MacBride.

WHEN TO GO:
Spring through fall.

INFORMATION:

Chamber of Commerce, P.O. Box 2358, Iowa City, Iowa
52240.

Amana Village Tours, P.O. Box 121, Amana, Iowa 52203

CAMPING:

Dakota Inn in Oxford. 3 miles south on 109 at Interstate 80.
56 sites. Showers, laundry, store.

Oxford Safari at jct 80 and 109. 143 sites. Showers, laundry,
store.

Near Solon: Lake MacBride State Park. 5 miles west on 382.
200 sites. Showers.

LODGING:

Holiday Inn of the Amana Colonies. Amana. Interstate 80 at
149. Restaurant, pool, store. 319/688-1175.

Colony House Motor Inn. State route 149, five miles south of
the Amana Colonies. 319/668-2097.

Old Capitol Inn, in Iowa City, U.S. 6 west of the city. Pool,
restaurant. 319/338-7901.

Hawkeye Lodge, Iowa City, U.S. 6 near campus. 319/338-
3651.

RESTAURANTS:

Bill Zuber's Dugout, Amana. 1 mile south of U.S. 6 at State
149.

Brat n'Brau Haus. 1 block north of U.S. 6 in South Amana.

Colony Market Place Restaurant, South Amana.

Old Homestead Inn and Rathskeller Lounge, Homestead.

Curt Yocum's, Iowa City, U.S. 6.

BIKE CARE:

Bicycle Pedalers, Iowa City. 319/338-9923.

Novotny's, Iowa City. 319/337-5525.

TRANSPORTATION:

Air service to Cedar Rapids. Train to Rock Island, Illinois.
Bus to Iowa City.

Amana Country Bike Trip Map

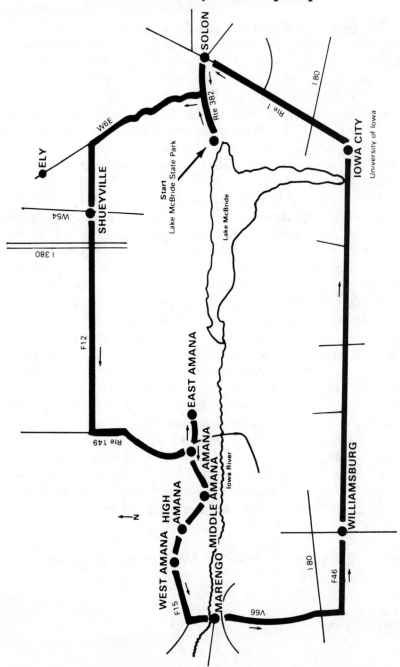

MISSISSIPPI ROUTE TO EFFIGY MOUNDS

This region of the state, called "Explorerland," is a place rich in the heritage of miners, trappers, hunters, and Indians. Biking along the Mississippi River, discover the history of these people, as well as some adventures of your own.

Iowa's northeast corner has natural scenic beauty. The climate is cooler here than in the rest of the state; there are high bluffs along the Mississippi, and many wooded areas. On this trip visit the Norwegian Museum and Festivals in Decorah, or the fascinating Effigy Mounds National Monument north of Marquette.

The mounds, which extend for three miles along the bluffs of the Mississippi River, are built in the shapes of animals and birds, and contain the remains of a prehistoric Indian culture that lived in the region 1,000 years ago. A visitor center offers a color slide program and museum exhibits which explain the history of the mounds. A self-guiding hiking trail tours the burial mounds, offers exhibits, and gives a lovely view of the river. It takes about 90 minutes of walking time and is open from 8 a.m. to 7 p.m. in the summer. Admission is free.

In Decorah, visit the Decorah Ice Cave at the northern edge of the town. A rare feature, it is one of the largest ice caves in the Midwest. Its walls and floor are coated from spring to mid-summer with ice. A feature of the Decorah park system, the cave provides cool relief if you get too hot after climbing those hills on your bike.

Ride along the Yellow River State Forest, located just inland from the Mississippi River near Waukon Junction and Harper's Ferry. Wildlife, a state-owned sawmill, pioneer farm buildings and unusual plant life can be found here.

LOCATION:
Northeast corner of Iowa in Winneshiek, Allamakee, and Clayton counties.

TERRAIN:
Hilly.

TRAVEL:
About 120 miles

TIME:
2–3 days.

ROAD SURFACE:
Paved. One mile gravel travel into Harper's Ferry.

TYPE OF TRIP:
Tour or camp.

ROUTE:
Begin at Decorah. Take County Road A52 east through Waukon 15 miles to X42, north to Lansing. At Lansing take X52 south to Harper's Ferry, along the Great River Road. Take 364 south to 76, south to Effigy Mounds National Monument (Marquette). Retrace 364 north to B45, west (to Monona) to X16, west and north to W4B, west along Yellow River to W60, north to A52, west to Decorah.

WHEN TO GO:
Spring through fall.

CAMPING:
Decorah Municipal Campground on U.S. 52. ¾ mile west of Jct 9. 80 sites. Showers. May 1–November 1.
Clear Creek Ranch, 2 miles west of Lansing on 9. 110 sites. Showers.
Pikes Peak State Park, 3 miles southeast of McGregor on 340. 125 sites. Showers, laundry, store.
Spook Cave Campground. 7 miles west of McGregor on 18, then 2 miles north, and follow signs. 100 sites. Store.
Gateway Park in Monona south of U.S. 18. 15 sites.

INFORMATION:
Decorah Chamber of Commerce, 102 E. Water St. 52101. 319/382-3990.

Mississippi Route to Effigy Mounds Map

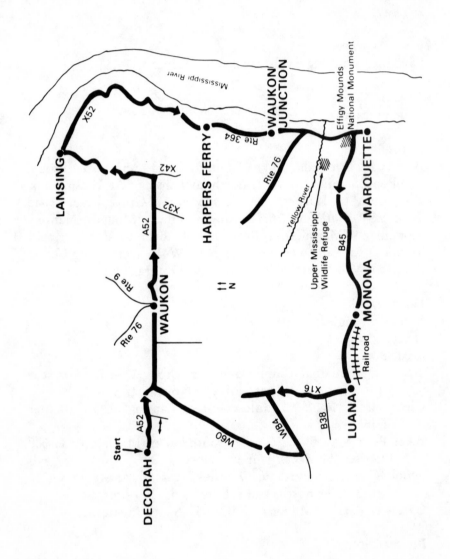

LODGING:

New Frontier Motel, Marquette, 20 units. Pool. On U.S. 18. 319/873-2396.

Pink Elephant Motel, Marquette. 18 units. Overlooks river. 319/873-3477.

Holiday Shores Motel in McGregor. 34 units. Pool. 319/873-3449.

Cliff House Motel in Decorah. Jct 9 and 55. 319/382-4241.

RESTAURANTS:

Pink Elephant in Marquette. Downtown on U.S. 76. Sweeping view of the Mississippi River.

Indian Isle in McGregor. On an island in the Mississippi River. Boat dock off U.S. 18.

BIKE CARE:

Monson Motors in Decorah. 319/382-5179.

Usgaard Smith in Decorah. 319/382-4864.

TRANSPORTATION:

Air service to Rochester, Minnesota. Bus to Decorah.

SPIRIT LAKE TRIP

The northwest area of Iowa, once a hunting and fishing land of the Sioux Indians, is a recreational area today, with several lakes surrounded by resort towns. Attractions are clear skies, blue waters and grasslands, village festivals, an unusual religious grotto, and a replica of a prairie fort.

Long before settlers came to the territory in 1856, this area, called the lakes region, had been a rendezvous for the Dakota tribes of the powerful Sioux, the Omahas, the Iowas, and the Yanktons. The lake the Indians called Spirit Water is now Spirit Lake, and Okoboji Lake means place of rest.

Four of Iowa's largest natural lakes are in Dickinson County: Spirit, East Okoboji, Silver, and West Okoboji. West Okoboji Lake is considered one of the three bluest lakes in the world. The other two are Lake Louise in Banff, Canada, and Lake Geneva in Switzerland.

On May 10, 1879, a meteorite fell on a farm two miles north of Estherville and broke into three large pieces which now reside in museums at the University of Minnesota; in Vienna, Austria; and in London, England.

Egralharve Mineral Spring, on the west side of West Okoboji Lake and just north of Vacation Village, is one of several springs in the Iowa Great Lakes Region. The water is supercharged with minerals. Life that is usually considered marine, and that is found nowhere else except in the Arctic Circle, is found in the spring.

Bike to Cayler Prairie, nine miles southwest of Spirit Lake, which is a natural prairie that is used as a study area by biologists because of its variety of prairie flowers and grasses.

Three miles southwest of Spirit Lake is a children's zoo called Deerland, with seals, bears, monkeys, birds, farm animals, and over 30 tame deer.

Other points of interest in the area are Kurious Kastle, a wildlife exhibit, Silver Lake Fen, a 15-acre fragile rare plant preserve, which you can view from the edges of the area, and Spirit Lake Fish Hatchery. Located on the isthmus between East Okoboji and Spirit Lake, the hatchery offers a slide show on spawning techniques, and you can see walleye and northern pike in holding pens.

LOCATION:
Northwestern Iowa in Dickinson County and southwestern Minnesota In Jackson County.

TERRAIN:
Flat.

TIME:
2-3 days.

ROAD SURFACE:
Paved.

TYPE OF TRIP:
Tour or camp.

WHEN TO GO:
Summer through fall.

ROUTE:
Begin at Fort Defiance campgrounds. Take A22 east (Estherville) to N26, north to N22, west and north into Minnesota to 276, south (Spirit Lake) to 9, west to 32, south to 71, south (Gardner Cabin) to A34, east to 203, south (Terrill) to N14, south to B17, east to N18, south and east (Lost Island Lake) to B25, east to N26, north to A34, west to N24, north to Fort Defiance.

CAMPING:
Acorn Ridge "Y" Camp 4 miles southeast of Spirit Lake on 56. 67 sites. Shower, laundry, store, lake swimming. May 1-October 15.
Arnold's Park. City park in town. 45 sites. Shower, store.
Orrs Camp Winakawin, ½ mile southeast of Arnold's Park off U.S. 71. 35 sites. Showers, lake swimming. May 1-October 1.
Red Arrow White Oak Campground. ½ mile south of Arnold's Park on 71. 45 sites. Showers, laundry, lake swimming. May 1-October 30.
Emersen Bay State Park, 2½ miles north of Mildford on 71. 32 sites. Swimming.
Gull Point State Park. 3 miles north of Milford on 32. 1 mile east. 250 sites. Shower, lake swimming. May 30-Labor Day.
Estherville City Park in town on 9. 10 sites.
Fort Defiance State Park, 1 mile south of Estherville on 9 then A22. 25 sites.

INFORMATION:
Chamber of Commerce, Arnold's Park C.E.O. Phil Hall, P.O. Box A, 51331. 712/332-2107.

Spirit Lake Trip Map

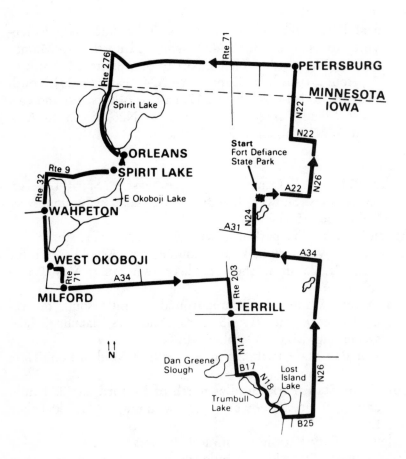

Estherville Chamber of Commerce, P.O. Box 435, 51334. 712/362-3541.

LODGING:

Oaks Motel, ½ mile east of 71 and 9 on East Okoboji Lake. 12 units. 712/336-2940.

Hotel Gardston, Estherville. Coffee shop. 712/362-2661.

Okoboji Brooks Beach Resort. Cottages and motel. Highway 71. Pool. 712/332-2955.

Fillenwarth New Beach Cottages on West Okoboji Lake. 70 units. Pool. 712/332-5646.

Palace Motel. Milford. Highway 71. 712/338-4701.

Trigg Lakeshore Motel. Arnold's Park. 28 units. Pool, sand beach. 712/332-2215.

RESTAURANTS:

The Black Coach. Route 71 North.

Teeg's Pink Slipper Steak House. State 32 South.

Tale n' Ale. ½ mile north on U.S. 71. 712/332-2982.

BIKE CARE:

Lakes, Lawn and Leisure in Spirit Lake. 712/336-2718.

South Town Sports in Arnold's Park. 712/332-2063.

TRANSPORTATION:

No train. Bus to Spirit Lake. Air service to Worthington, Minnesota, 31 miles north.

8

Michigan: Introduction and Trails

State Capital: Lansing
State Flower: Apple Blossom
State Tree: White Pine
State Bird: Robin
State Nickname: "Wolverine State"

Michigan is the kind of place where it's hard to stop biking once you start because just 10 miles north or south or east or west, there's another spectacular sight—whether it be water-falls, dunes, hills, rivers, virgin timber, or deserted lake shoreline.

Driving on Interstate 94 between Chicago and Detroit in the southern part of the state, you get the impression that Michigan blends into one huge suburban area. This impression is somewhat accurate in the bottom third of the Lower Peninsula. But even here, there are some lovely rural areas to bike.

When in Michigan, don't miss Holland's famous tulips.

Sixty percent of the nation's motor vehicles are made in the Detroit area because of Michigan's wealth of raw materials and the superb transportation on the Great Lakes. Yet the Upper and Lower peninsulas of this state offer varied bicycling country. Trips can range from easy, level rides around bright lakes and through resort towns with lots of tourist attractions in the Lower Peninsula, to rugged rides through unspoiled forests in the Upper Peninsula, where the only other life you may meet on the road is a black bear.

There is plenty of space for a cyclist to rest and camp in Michigan's three national forests and 29 state forests, which together have 229 campgrounds. And the state's total coastline is second only to Alaska's, with 11,000 lakes and 36,000 miles of river and streams, which puts the cyclist within 20 minutes of water, wherever he bikes. Over 700 registered historical sites, and Mackinac Island, which allows no motor vehicles on it, make interesting two wheeled excursions. Mackinac Bridge is a five-mile-long engineering wonder also worth taking a look at.

Tourism is one of the state's top three industries, so the state gives strong support to bikers and has many active bike clubs. Private accommodations for the bike tripper are readily available, and many county and township parks can be used for camping. You can route excellent trips on the 88,000 miles of county roads, with scen c or recreational destinations. For free county maps, up to a quantity of 12, write the following address (allow three weeks for delivery):

> Department of State Highways and Transportation
> Bike Maps
> P. O. Box 30050
> Lansing, Michigan 48909

Made up of the Upper and Lower Peninsulas, Michigan touches the shores of four of the five Great Lakes. The name, "Michigan," means "large lake" in the Algonquin Indian language.

In the western part of the Upper Peninsula, one of the world's richest mining regions has vast deposits of copper and iron. Nevertheless the peninsula is not all raked with mining scars. It is a hilly land of rapid rivers, waterfalls, lakes, and forests. In the Huron Mountains of the northern Marquette and Baraga counties, the land elevation reaches over 1,900 feet above sea level. Further west, Michigan's highest point of 1,980 feet is located in the Porcupine Mountains. Some highways here, such as U.S. 31, have a biker's lane, which is greatly appreciated by cyclists, for Michigan traffic is often heavy.

If you bike camp in the Upper Peninsula, be careful of bears that roam freely. Hang all your food away from your tent at least eight feet off the ground between two trees, and don't bring food into your tent at any time! Generally bears are not a nuisance but if you happen upon one don't try to outrun it on foot. Stand still, for motion excites them. If they get too close, lie on your stomach on the ground and play dead. Many people say that since bears are color blind, you blend into the background if you don't move. And, of course, keep quiet.

The eastern portion of the Upper Peninsula is low, with sand dunes and miles and miles of national shoreline along Lake Superior which has no development and not a soul on it. You must be a strong biker to ride along the Lake Superior shoreline, and be willing to walk your bike at times, for the roads are unpaved. But the seasoned biker will find that the serenity and beauty is worth it as he rides through picturesque villages, past old lighthouses, and fishing villages, and around stunning waterfalls.

You pass the magnificent Tahquamenon Falls near Newberry, which is the largest of 150 waterfalls in the Upper Peninsula. Legend says that Hiawatha lived here, and the falls are immortalized in Longfellow's poem, "The Song of Hiawatha."

Tahquamenon Falls is about a day's bike ride west of Sault Ste. Marie. At the Lower Tahquamenon Falls you can rent a boat and paddle in the Tahquamenon River around the small islands. This river flows into Lake Superior just below Whitefish Point.

Watch boats pass through the busy Soo Locks, which annually handle more traffic than the Panama and the Suez canals combined.

Highway 28 cuts through the center of the Upper Peninsula and is paved, as is Highway 2, which runs along the Lake Michigan shoreline in the southern part of the peninsula. Both of these roads make good bike tour routes. For information on the Upper Peninsula, write:

Travel and Recreation Association
P. O. Box 400
Iron Mountain, Michigan 49801
Phone: 906/774-5480

Michigan has a longer shoreline than any state except Alaska.

Michigan's Lower Peninsula is a level plain with some highlands, rolling hills, sand dunes, and swamps. The long growing season and rich soil make it an important agricultural area. Many lakes formed by glaciers and surrounded by forests make it a popular recreational area. More than half the state is wooded, and wild strawberries, raspberries, huckleberries, and elderberries grow throughout the region.

Shifting sand dunes, sometimes piling as high as 600 feet, are found in the northwestern corner of the Lower Peninsula. In the north central part of the peninsula, a sandy highland rises to more than 1,000 feet.

Many cultural and recreational attractions in the state are worth seeing. The country's finest display of early American life was collected by Henry Ford and is on view at Greenfield Village in Dearborn. Greenfield Village also has a stern-wheel riverboat that is nearly 100 years old.

Mackinac Island, at the northern tip of the peninsula, becomes a sailboat racing center in late summer. No cars are allowed on the island, and it is a popular biking spot. All kinds of bikes can be rented on the island.

For travel brochures and information on historic and other sights, festivals and events, as well as camping information, write:

> Michigan Travel Commission
> Lansing, Michigan 48913
> Phone: 517/373-1195

The American Youth Hostels (AYH) Bike Route Atlas has 28 maps and shows 1,200 miles of biking in the Detroit metropolitan area. Send a $2.00 money order to:

> Metropolitan Detroit Council
> American Youth Hostels
> 3024 Coolidge Road
> Berkley, Michigan 48072

The Automobile Club of Michigan publishes a series of 16 bike tours in various parts of the state. These maps are free. The routes pass through scenic countryside and points of interest, but are, at times, routed over roads with heavy traffic. For information write:

> Touring Department
> Automobile Club of Michigan
> 139 Bagley Avenue
> Detroit, Michigan 48126

A superior set of bicycle tours in nine areas in western Michigan are available from the Michigan Department of Natural Resources, complete with maps and mileage. Called *Biking Western Michigan,* you can receive this packet of tours free by writing:

Michigan Department of Natural Resources
Box 30028
Lansing, Michigan 48909

As you ride along the shorelines and forests of this state, you'll experience some of the wonder and adventure that explorers, trappers, traders, and missionaries knew when they opened the state for settlement. For even today, much of Michigan is tranquil wilderness.

MICHIGAN BIKE RULES

Bicyclists have the same rights and duties as do drivers of other vehicles in this state. However, cyclists are not allowed to ride on freeways, and when separate and useable bicycle paths are available, cyclists must use these paths instead of the roadway. Bikers may not ride more than two abreast, except on bike paths, and must have a light that can be seen from 500 feet at night. A bell that can be heard 100 feet away is also required, but no sirens or whistles can be used by a biker.

HOLLAND TRAIL

Start this easy, two-day trip at Saugatuck on the Lake Michigan shoreline, about 23 miles south of Holland. At Saugatuck take a paddle wheel boat cruise, visit an art colony, or ride dune schooners over the sands. Begin the trip along Kalamazoo Lake, and bike up to Lake Macatawa and Holland, a city of tulips, wooden shoes, and windmills. In early May celebrate the Tulip Festival, enjoy hundreds of thousands of brightly colored flowers, watch Klompen Dancers, parades, pageants, hear organ recitals, and see authentic Dutch costumes worn by the villagers, who scrub down the streets. The Dutch settled this town in 1847, and today the townspeople celebrate their heritage with acres of tulips, a wooden shoe factory, a Dutch Village, and Netherlands Museum.

"De Zwaan," a 200-year-old windmill transplanted from a

A group of cyclists enjoying the Lake Michigan shoreline.

dairy field in the Netherlands to a city park, Windmill Island, on the Black River in Holland, is open to the public. Admission is free except during Tulip Time in May. The 10-story mill, which was shipped in 7,000 pieces and reassembled by a Dutch millwright, is surrounded by a tulip bed of 150,000 blossoms.

Dutch farmers started the fruit industry in this part of the state, and made Grand Rapids the leading furniture center of the nation. Holland has the only furniture museum in the country which has displays of furniture from early colonial days to the present.

Just northeast of Holland, the town of Zeeland has an 8½-mile bicycle pathway which encompasses sites of historical interest, such as the Settler's Monument, and historic old homes.

Tour the Vander Burgh Art Studio, a stained glass window manufacturing company, in Zeeland. It is opened Monday through Friday, 8:30 a.m. to 5:30 p.m., and Saturdays until noon. Phone 616/772-4312.

LOCATION:
Allegan and Ottawa counties in southwestern Michigan.

TERRAIN:
Flat to rolling hills.

TRAVEL:
About 60 miles.

TIME:
One or two days.

ROAD SURFACE:
Paved.

TYPE OF TRIP:
Day, tour, or camp.

ROUTE:
Begin in Saugatuck. Take Washington St. north to 65th St., north to Shore Drive, east around Lake Macatawa to Beach Road, west around north shore of same lake to 152nd St., north to Lakewood, west to Lake Shore, (along Lake Michigan) north around Pigeon Lake past Kirk Park & Lake Michigan St. and past Buchanan St. At the next blacktop road going east turn right to Lincoln St., east to 144th Ave., north to Green St., east to Cedar Drive (along the Grand River), east to 104th Ave., south to Lincoln St., east to Warner, east to 68th St., south into Allendale and on to Fillmore, west to 72nd Ave., south to Chicago Drive, west through Zeeland to 112th St., south to Adams St., west to Shore Drive, west around Lake Macatawa's southern shoreline to 64th St., south back to Saugatuck.

WHEN TO GO:
Spring through fall. May during Tulip Festival Time.

CAMPING:
Holland State Park. Ottawa Beach Road, Holland, 49423. 616/335-8959. Two campgrounds. Lake Michigan and Lake Macatawa. 342 sites. Showers.

Vehdheer's Tulip Gardens. 3 miles north on U.S. 31, then 100 feet east on Quincy. 50 sites. May 1–October 1.

West Wind Resort in Saugatuck. Off I-196 at Exit 41, then ½ mile west on Blue Star Highway. 145 sites. Showers, laundry, store, 616/857-2528.

INFORMATION:
Holland Chamber of Commerce, Civic Center, 7 East 8th St. 49423. 616/392-2389. For motel and camping reservations call: 616/396-4191.

Zeeland Chamber of Commerce, 39 Maple St. 49464.

The Holland Chamber of Commerce will send you an excellent, large, colored map of Ottawa County with paved and unpaved roads marked on it. Ask for the Ottawa County Road Map.

LODGING:
Wooden Shoe. 16th Street at U.S. 31, Holland. Heated pool. 616/392-8521.

Ship n' Shore. 528 Water Street, Saugatuck. 616/587-2188.

RESTAURANTS:
Dutch Village. Located inside the Dutch Village, which charges entrance fees. Dutch Cuisine. April 15 through October 15. Holland.

Beechwood Inn on Ottawa Beach Road, Holland. 6a.m.-8p.m. 616/396-2355.

Copper Kettle. 139 East 8th Street, Holland.

Village Inn Pizza. 934 S. Washington. Sing-along Friday and Saturday nights. Holland. 616/392-1818.

Bosch's Restaurant. 120 E. Main St., Zeeland 49464.

Holland Trail Map

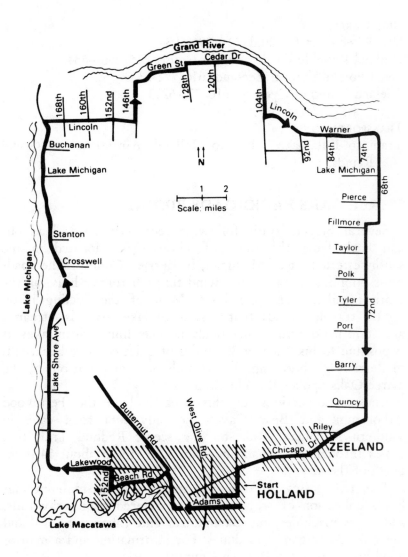

Van Raalte's Restaurant. 202 E. Main St., Zeeland 49464.
Community Kitchens Inc. 421 E. Main St., Zeeland 49464.
Dionese Confectionery. 134 East Main St., Zeeland 49464.

BIKE CARE:
Highwheeler in Holland. 616/396-6084.
Holland Reliable Cycle and Ski House. 616/396-4684.
Pedal Power Shop in Zeeland. 616/772-2333.
Zeeland Schwinn Cyclery. 616/772-6223.

TRANSPORTATION:
Train to Kalamazoo. Bus to Holland. Air service to Grand
    Rapids.

THREE OAKS BACKROADS BIKEWAY

Several bicycle trails following secondary roads lead out
and back from the town of Three Oaks, located in the
southwestern part of Michigan, in Berrien County. The roads
cross bubbling streams, and wind through rolling hills, patchwork farmland, and meadows. Most of the cycling is on
lightly traveled roads that pass small lakes, woods, streams,
and state parks with white sandy beaches lining clean lakes. It
is possible to bike nearly 300 miles of quiet country backroads
in Berrien by following all the trails on a map put out by the
Three Oaks Spokes Bicycle Club.

Unusual attractions in this area include the Fernwood
Arboretum and Bear Cave, the only tufa rock cave in
southern Michigan. Ride on the scenic Redbud Trail that
passes through Buchanan and joins U.S. 13/33 about 14 miles
north of the city.

This trip passes forest hiking trails, a steam museum that
has a collection of working steam-powered trains, sawmills,
and other machines, the Baumholzer and Tabor wineries, and
the Lake Michigan sand dunes. For information and a map of
good biking roads in Berrien County, write:

> Three Oaks Spokes Bicycle Club
> Three Oaks, Michigan

Camp near towering sand dunes at Warren Dunes, where you can take hang gliding lessons on weekdays for a fee, or just watch daredevils with huge kites strapped to their backs soar into the air when the wind is right.

A quarter mile south of Warren Dunes, turn off the Red Arrow Highway, and ride into wine country. From here, it is a 12 mile ride to the Tabor Hill winery, via Gardner and Mt. Tabor roads.

At the Tabor Hill Vineyard, located on Tabor Hill Road, wine making tours are conducted in the facility which is nestled in an orchard where the grapes are grown. The 40-minute tours, offered from noon to 5:30 p.m. daily, include sampling any wine in the house.

From Tabor Hill, take a five mile ride via Mt. Tabor, Snow Road, and the Red Bud Trail, through picturesque vineyards and along the winding St. Joseph River to Bear Cave Resort north of Buchanan. Amateur spelunkers can take a half-hour guided tour of the cavern for a fee on weekdays, daily from Memorial Day to Labor Day and on weekends from Labor Day to November 1. Year-round temperature in the cave is a cool 58 degrees.

Bear Cave Resort has a general store, camping facilities, canoe rental, and picnicking on the banks of the St. Joseph River.

In addition to orchards and vineyards, canoeing on the quiet St. Joseph, or swimming in Lake Michigan, visit the Cook Nuclear Reactor, which gives free 45-minute presentations on electricity and nuclear energy. Browse among the exhibits, one of which is a wristwatch-sized television. The Donald C. Cook Nuclear Power Plant is located on a bluff overlooking Lake Michigan, just north of Bridgeman.

In fall, see the Four Flags Apple Festival in Niles, Michigan, with apple parades, a carnival, and many other attractions. For information write:

Apple Festival
Box 762
Niles, Michigan 49120
Phone: 616/684-1965

LOCATION:
Southwestern Michigan in Berrien County.

TERRAIN:
Moderately hilly.

TRAVEL:
About 65 miles.

TIME:
One or two days.

ROAD SURFACE:
Paved.

TYPE OF TRIP:
Day, tour, or camp.

ROUTE:
Begin trip at Warren Dunes. Take the Red Arrow Highway
    south to Browntown Road, east to Snow Road, north and
    east to Jericho Road, north to Linco Road, east to Jericho
    Road, north to Johnson Road to town of Stevensville.
    Take First St. south to Hills Road, south and east to
    Snow Road, south and east to Tabor Hill Winery. Take
    Snow Road east to West Ferry St. (in Berrien Springs).
    Take Ferry east to U.S. 31/33, south and east to Range
    Line Road, southwest to Synder Road (Lake Chapin
    Wayside), west to Range Line Road, south to Walton
    Road, west to Fourth St., west (1 block) to Main St.
    (Buchanan, for food and bike repair). Take Buchanan St.
    west to Cleveland St., north to Warren Woods Road,
    west to Flynn Road, north to Browntown Road, west to
    Red Arrow Highway, north to Warren Dunes State Park.

WHEN TO GO:
Spring through fall. Orchards in flower in the spring; Lake

Michigan swimming in summer; beautiful colorama in fall.

INFORMATION:

Buchanan Chamber of Commerce, 119 Main St., 49107. 616/695-3291.

Berrien Springs Chamber of Commerce, 110 West Ferry St., 49103. 616/471-5311.

Niles Chamber of Commerce, 616/683-3720.

West Michigan Tourist Association, 136 Fulton East, Grand Rapids, Michigan 49502. 616/456-8557.

Cook Nuclear Center, Bridgeman. Free theatre presentations. Wednesday through Saturday, 10 a.m. to 5 p.m., and Sunday, noon to 6 p.m. 616/465-6101.

Tours of local wineries can be arranged by contacting:

Tabor Hill Vineyard, Buchanan. 616/422-1515.

Lakeside Vineyard and Winery, Harbert (five miles south of Warren Dunes on the lake). 616/469-0700.

Bronte Wine Company, Keeler (25 miles northeast of Berrien Springs). 616/621-3419.

CAMPING:

Warren Dunes State Park, on Lake Michigan. 249 sites. Lake swimming, showers. For camping reservations for no less than four nights, call 15 days in advance. 616/426-4013.

Oronoko Lakes in Berrien Springs. 4½ miles west on Snow Road. 25 sites. Showers, store.

Bear Cave in Buchanan. 4 miles north on the Red Bud Trail. 72 sites. Showers, store, swimming pool. May 1-November 1.

Three Braves in Buchanan. 1½ miles west of Front St., then two miles northwest on Madron Lake Road. 1½ mile northwest on Wagner Road, one mile west on Abel Road. 75 sites. Showers, store. May 1-October 1.

Fullers Resort at Clear Lake. 120 sites. Swimming.

LODGING:

Golden Eagle Inn in Niles, 4 miles east of Buchanan on

Three Oaks Backroads Bikeway Map

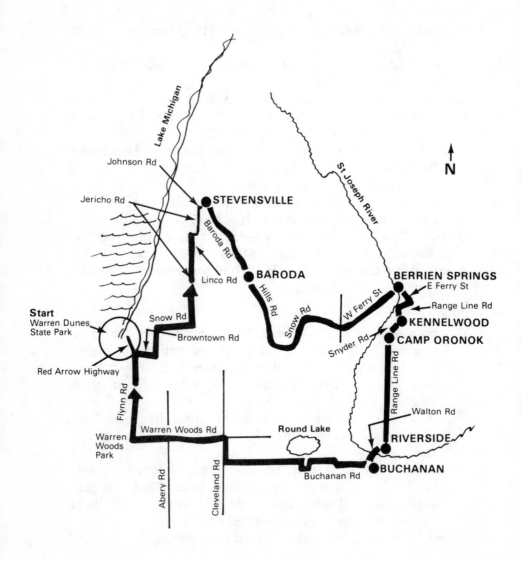

Buchanan Road. 1243 S. 11th St. Heated pool. 616/684–
1000.

BIKE CARE:
Cycle Path, Stevensville. 616/429-4483.
Gamble's Store, Buchanan. 616/695-6891.

TRANSPORTATION:
Air service to Benton Harbor and Kalamazoo, bus to Benton
Harbor, train to Niles.

MANISTEE FOREST TRIP

Manistee is an Indian word for "Spirit of the Woods," and
you'll get to know this spirit as you bike through forests of
second growth hardwoods, poplar, and pine. This moderately
hilly route through forests and along lakes and rivers has few
stores or service stations, so you ought to be self-sufficient.
Carry enough food, water, and snacks to get you through the
day, as well as tools for any likely bike breakdowns. There is
plenty of shade on the tree-lined roads, and the ride is tops in
pleasure for bikers seeking the peace, solitude, and beauty of
nature. Some of Michigan's finest scenery in the Lower
Peninsula is around this area. Seasoned riders can make this
trip in a day; children and leisurely bikers will want to make
an overnight stop at camping facilities along the route.

State and federal forest lands comprise much of the trip.
You can camp on any lands not posted with signs that say "no
camping" in these areas. Farms are primarily dairy, fruit, and
small truck farms. Fishing for rainbow trout, brown trout, and
steelheads on this part of the Manistee River is excellent.
There are several public access fishing sites.

Atop a high hill in Ludington a huge cross marks the spot
where explorer Père Marquette died in 1675. Ludington State
Park, where you begin, has miles of sandy beach both along
Lake Michigan and along Hamlin Lake. The city of Ludington
is a port for car and passenger ferry service across Lake
Michigan to Wisconsin.

The American Salmon Derby is headquartered at Ludington each summer, and the Rose Hawley Museum in the downtown area has displays from Ludington's past.

Increase the mileage of this trip by hooking up with route 31 along the Lake Michigan shoreline and riding north, all the way up to Sleeping Bear Dunes State Park, if you like.

LOCATION:
Michigan Lower Peninsula in Mason and Lake counties.

TERRAIN:
Hilly.

TRAVEL:
90 miles.

TIME:
2 days.

ROAD SURFACE:
Paved.

TYPE OF TRIP:
Day, tour, or camp.

WHEN TO GO:
Summer through fall.

ROUTE:
Begin at Ludington State Park. Take 116 to Shore Drive, 2 miles north to Dewey. Two miles east to Lakewood Drive, north to Angling Road, northeast to Fountain Road, east 10 miles to village of Fountain. Take Reek Road north to Beger (jog east and north around Gun Lake) to Freesoil Road 10 miles east to Bass Lake Road (2 miles north is a campground on the Little Manistee River). Bass Lake Road south 3½ miles to Loon Lake Road, 1 mile west to Hamilton, 5½ miles south to

Back roads
are the best
for bike riding—
and they're also
more scenic.

Centerline Road, 2 miles west to North Branch Road, 3
miles south to U.S. 10 (busy—ride carefully) 4½ miles
west (through Walhalla) to Benson Road, 4 miles north to
Round Lake (camping) to Sugar Grove Road, 10 miles
west to Stiles Road, south to Hanson Road, west to
Rassmussen Road, west to Lakewood, north to Dewey,
west to Lake Shore Drive to 116, north to Ludington
State Park.

CAMPING:

Ludington State Park. 398 sites. Showers, beach swimming,
snack bar. North of Ludington on Lake Shore Drive 2½
miles, then northwest on 116 three miles.

Crystal Lake Campgrounds. 5¾ miles east on U.S. 10. 1½

miles north on Stiles Road. ½ mile east on Hanson Road. 79 sites. Showers, store, lake swimming. May 1–October 1.

Lakeview Campgrounds. 2 miles east on U.S. 10. 4¾ miles north on Jebavy Road. 2½ miles northeast on Angling Road. ⅛ mile east on Fountain Road. 1½ mile north on Peterson Road. 32 sites. Showers, stores. April 1–November 1.

Pump Storage Campground. 5½ miles south on U.S. 31 then 1½ mile west on Chauvez Road. 37 sites. Showers.

Meadow Campsites near Scottsville. 8 miles north on U.S. 31. 40 sites. Showers. May 1–November 30.

INFORMATION:

Ludington Chamber of Commerce, Box 247, 49431. 616/843-2506.

LODGING:

Viking Arms. 930 East Ludington. 616/843-3441.

Big Log Cabin Resort. On south shore of Round Lake, 3 miles north of Walhalla. 616/462-3218.

Candlewyck Village Motel on U.S. 10, ¾ mile west of U.S. 31 at 1001 East Ludington Avenue. 616/843-3631.

Peter's Edgewater Resort on Upper Hamlin Lake, 9 miles north of Ludington. 616/843-2176.

RESTAURANTS:

Gibbs Country House Restaurant. 3951 West U.S. 10, east of city. Home baked bread. 616/845-5086. Ludington.

Scotty's Harbor House. On East Ludington Avenue (U.S. 10) one mile east of downtown Ludington. Swedish pancakes. April through December. 616/843-4033.

BIKE CARE:

The Other Bicycle Shop in Ludington (Schwinn Dealer). 616/845-7146.

Manistee Trail Map

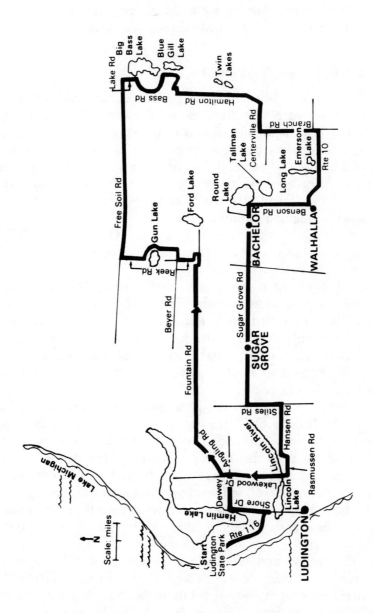

TRANSPORTATION:
Ferry across Lake Michigan from Wisconsin to Ludington. Bus
to Ludington. Air service to Manistee, Michigan (25 miles
north on Lake). Bus to Manistee, Michigan.

ALPENA TO OCQUEOC TRAIL

In this area mushrooming is considered an outdoor sport.
Towns have such appellations as Polaski and Posen, and
mailboxes bear names of Russian and Polish Americans. You
may get the feeling you're biking in the Old Country, as you
pass houses isolated from one another by forests of birch, oak,
and pine growing close together. As you follow the dips and
curves of this fairly flat trip you may half expect to see a
troika with laughing children in it.

In the middle 1800s large groups of German and Polish
immigrants settled in and around Rogers City, but their
culture is just one part of the area's lore.

Even before their arrival, in 1668, Father Marquette sent
missionaries into these woods. The Indians told the "Black
Robes," as they called the priests, the legend of Sacred Rock.
Located six miles north of Rogers City, this rock is the site
where two Indian chiefs fought, and were struck and killed by
lightning. According to the myth, when it rains, you can see
their blood on the rocks.

The area has a fascinating geology and economy as well as
history. At Rogers City, the mammoth Calcite Quarry is the
largest quarrying operation in the world. There are two
lookout stations at the quarry. Quarry View overlooks the
operations, which were begun in 1912, and Harbor View
affords a panorama of self-loading ships entering and leaving
the harbor. There is a fossil collection in the office, and guides
will answer questions about the five-mile-long, three-mile-
wide enterprise.

At the intersection of Maple and Leer on your route there
is a prehistoric sinkhole—a pit about 150 feet deep formed by
the interaction of water with limestone. Sink holes are found
in a 50 mile line from Thunder Bay to Black Lake. Some dry

sinkholes in Alpena County can be 300 feet in diameter. These holes form when rainwater seepage dissolves the limestone bedrock, and caves form underground. The cave roofs eventually collapse to form sinkholes. There are about 200 sinkholes in northeastern Michigan. Unusual ferns and mosses grow in these cool, dark sinks.

For a map of the Black Lake State Forest sinkholes foot trail at Shoepac Lake in Presque Isle County, write the Rogers City Chamber of Commerce.

Take swimsuits on this trip, for it follows the shoreline of Lake Huron before turning inland to Lower Michigan's largest waterfall, Ocqueoc Falls. You can swim in the lake or dive into the cascading falls. Ocqueoc, which meant "sacred" to the Chippewa Indians, has two falls 300 feet apart, and fine campgrounds.

There's lots of free time happiness on this trip. In Alpena, visit the wildfowl sanctuary and feed corn to the birds, or stop at the Jesse Besser Museum, named for the industrialist who developed the first concrete block machine. The museum has an avenue of 1890 shops, a fence made of iron ore, and a bow anchor, taken from the steamer Pewabic, which sank off Thunder Bay Island in 1865. Three 19th century buildings have been moved to the museum grounds.

At Old Presque Isle Lighthouse, learn how to "shoot the sun" with an old brass sextant, play a pump organ, find out about area shipwrecks, or climb up the hand-chiseled stone staircase of the 1840 lighthouse. Lighthouse attendants are on duty from 8 a.m. to 10 p.m. Memorial Day through Labor Day.

Presque Isle County is 77 percent forest, most of which is an undeveloped wilderness with motels and resorts that draw vacationers. The county is proud of its reputation as an ideal climate for hay fever sufferers—it has one of the lowest pollen counts in the state.

Alpena, once a lumbering center, made the transition to limestone around 1837. It is also a resort town with summer activities that include an annual CB Jamboree, Memorial Day and Fourth of July parades and festivities, outdoor art shows,

Brown Trout Festival, and the county fair. Part of its appeal is due to the fact that it has the mildest climate of any city in the state. Located in the heart of the lake region and on Thunder Bay, it has high winter and low summer temperatures. Prevailing winds blow cool, water-washed breezes in from Lake Huron in the summer, so bring warm clothing.

At Posen, participate in the potato festival in September, or swim and camp in Fletcher County Park, southwest of the town.

LOCATION:
Lower Peninsula of Michigan, northeast corner, Presque Isle and Alpena counties.

TERRAIN:
Moderately hilly.

TRAVEL:
125 miles.

TIME:
4 days.

ROAD SURFACE:
Paved except for some smooth gravel on the way to Presque Isle Lighthouse. Two miles of smooth, well-graded gravel on 638 with nice view of forests.

TYPE OF TRIP:
Tour or camp.

ROUTE:
Begin in Alpena. Take U.S. 23 north to Grand Lake Road, north to Presque Isle Lighthouse. Take 405 south to 638 (gravel then paved), north to 23, west and north to Rogers City. Take 68 west to Ocqueoc Falls. Take 68 south to Millerburg Road, south to 638, east to 451, south to 634, east to Leer Road, south to Maple Lane Road, east to 65, south to 32, east to Alpena.

WHEN TO GO:
Spring through fall.

CAMPING:
Beaver Lake County Park in Alpena. 16 miles west on 32, 8 miles south on 65, then 1½ mile west on Beaver Lake Road. 54 sites. Showers, lake swimming. Memorial Day–Labor Day.

Long Lake County Park. 11 miles north of Alpena on U.S. 23 then ½ mile west on Park Road. 85 sites. Showers, lake swimming.

Thunder Bay River Campground. 7 miles west on 32. Three miles south on County Road. 15 sites.

Hoeft Campgrounds. 5 miles northwest of Rogers City off U.S. 23. 146 sites. Showers, store, lake swimming.

Ocqueoc Falls Campground. 12 miles west on 68. 12 sites.

INFORMATION:
Alpena Chamber of Commerce, P.O. Box 65, 49707. 517/354-4181.

Rogers City Chamber of Commerce, P.O. Box 55, 49779. 514/734-2535.

LODGING:
Parker House in Alpena. U.S. 23 at State 5. 12 miles north of town. 517/595-6484.

Falkner's Landing in Alpena. M-32 west. 517/354-5973.

Woody's Resort, 4709 Long Rapids Road, Alpena. 517/356-0127.

Presque Isle Motel, 385 N. Bradley Highway, Rogers City, 49779. 517/734-4060.

Vogler's Tourist Home, 385 S. Third Street, Rogers City. 517/734-2985.

International Hotel, 192 East Huron Avenue, Rogers City. 517/734-9009.

RESTAURANTS:
A & W Drive-In, 1032 U.S. 23 North, Alpena. 517/356-9991.
The Grove, U.S. 23 North, Alpena. 517/354-4191.

Alpena to Ocqueoc Trail Map

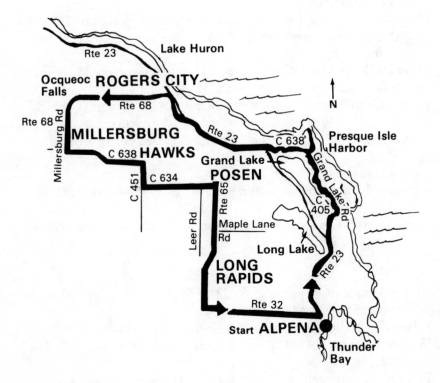

Harvest Table Restaurant, 122 W. Chisholm St. 517/354-8523.

Reuben Haus, 2261 U.S. 23 South, Alpena. 517/354-3535.

Roostertail Dining Room. 390 S. First St. 9 a.m.-9p.m. Sundays and holidays, noon to 8 p.m. Closed Monday from mid-January to mid-April. Rogers City. 517/734-3123.

Karsten's Dairy, 1072 W. Third St., Rogers City. 517/734-2050.

BIKE CARE:

Cobblestone City Bike Dealer, Alpena. 517/356-1238.

TRANSPORTATION:

Air service to Alpena. Bus to Alpena and Rogers City. No trains.

HOUGHTON TO COPPER HARBOR TRIP

Fort Wilkins, at the tip of this peninsula, has been a popular bikers' haven for nearly 100 years. As early as 1880, the Lake Superior Bicycle Club had regular outings to the fort, which is three miles east of the town of Copper Harbor. At that time, it was used as a resort, and turkey shoots, band music, dances and other festivities were held there.

Built in 1844 to protect the settlers of Copper Harbor from an imaginary Indian threat, the fort was never used militarily. Today it has been reconstructed to some degree, and is a good example of a mid-19th century military outpost, with a bakehouse, barracks, mess hall, officers' quarters, ice house, powder magazine, and more. Take a ferry to the Copper Harbor Lighthouse, built in 1866.

There is much more than the fort on this trip up the Keweenaw peninsula, which juts out into Lake Superior. Solitude and beautiful country combine with an abundance of copper mining and ethnic history to make this trip unique. It passes rocky shorelines, sandy beaches, placid inland lakes, and miles of thick forests. Be self-sufficient, for there are few restaurants, stores or motels out of Houghton until you reach

Copper Harbor. Concessions in Copper Harbor tend to be expensive.

Fall colors approach their peak beginning September 28, and reach their peak around October 10. The woods are breathtaking at this time, particularly on drives such as the Gay Road, from Lac La Belle to Lake Linden, Brockway Mountain Drive, which runs along U.S. 41 from Delaware to Copper Harbor, route M-203 from Hancock to Calumet, the Arboreal Tunnel west of Houghton, and the lookout atop Quincy Hill. To find out about the status of the colors each week, call the Copper Country Chamber of Commerce at 906/482-5240.

For information on an autumn vacation write:

> Copper Country Vacation
> Box 336 HK
> Houghton, Michigan 49931

Portage Lake was used by the Indians, who cut through the peninsula, and then portaged their canoes a mile to Lake Superior on the west side. The name of this county, Keweenaw, means, "Place where we make short cut on foot."

As you near Torch Lake, the reddish hue of the waters is a reminder of the tons of reclaimed copper sands (tailings) dumped into its water. For information write:

> Torch Lake Chamber of Commerce
> Lake Linden, Michigan 49945

Prehistoric men, Chippewa Indians, and finally, European white men lived on this peninsula, mined the ore, fished, and hunted. In the early mining days in the 1840s over 90 percent of the labor force came from Europe, bringing their traditions with them. Two ethnic groups maintain especially strong identities here, the Cornish people, who came from the mines of Cornwall, and Finnish immigrants, who came to till the soil. This area is the center of Finnish culture in America.

The climate is much like that of their homeland; in late summer the weather is cool and many of the trees begin to change. One advantage of biking here is that the humidity on the peninsula is quite low, making the few hot days tolerable and the cold days not as chilling as damp cold days.

There are many mines, both active and inactive, in the area. At the Quincy Mine in Hancock, the world's largest steam operated mine hoist is housed in a building four stories high. At the Arcadian mine at Ripley you enter through a hillside adit (horizontal opening in a mountain) and travel 300 feet below the surface of the earth. The Delaware mine dates back to 1847 and is near a ghost town. Copper from this region has been pushed by glaciers as far south as Chicago.

Coppertown U.S.A. in Calumet is a historic mining, educational, ethnic and tourist complex developed in the former Calumet and Hecla Mining Company Headquarters. It has a museum, exhibitions, festivals and shops. For information write:

> Coppertown U.S.A.
> 101 Red Jacket Road
> Calumet, Michigan 49913

Copper was also responsible for the founding of the Michigan Technological University in Houghton. Portage Lake and the Huron Mountains form a scenic backdrop for this school.

These are only a few of the many historic sites you can visit on your trip through this northern wilderness. Or you can bypass them entirely, and pedal peacefully along tree-shaded highways that alternately skirt sand dunes, lakes, rivers, and forests.

LOCATION:
Upper Peninsula of Michigan, northwest section. Keweenaw and Houghton counties.

TERRAIN:
Moderately hilly.

TRAVEL:
110 miles.

Water—the best thirst-quencher for a hot cyclist.

TIME:
3–4 days.

ROAD SURFACE:
Paved.

TYPE OF TRIP:
Tour or camp.

ROUTE:
Begin in Houghton. Take M203 10 miles northwest along
    canal to Lake Superior shoreline. Take 203 east (into
    Calumet) to 41, north (to Ahmeek) to Cliff Drive, north
    to (Phoenix) 26, northwest then northeast along sand
    dunes and Lake Superior shoreline to Eagle Harbor to
    Brockway Mountain Drive, east to Copper Harbor and
    Fort Wilkins. Backtrack 26, west 3 miles from Fort
    Wilkins to Copper Harbor to 41, west to paved road

leading southeast to Lac La Belle. Take only paved road southeast and then north around Lac La Belle to Point Isabelle and down the eastern coastline of the peninsula. At the town of Gay take only paved road west to Mohawk and U.S. 41, south (to Laurium) to 26, east and south and then west to Houghton.

WHEN TO GO:
Spring through fall.

CAMPING:
Fort Wilkins State Park. Copper Harbor. 165 sites. Shower, refreshments. 906/289-4215.
Staton Township Park. North Canal Road, Houghton 49931. Primitive campsite. Free.
Gordon Robert Campground. Tamrack Location, Calumet, U.S. 41. Water. 906/523-4122.
McLain State Park. 7 miles west of Calumet on M203. 91 sites. Showers, groceries, beach. 906/482-0278.
Lake Fanny Hooe Resort and Campgrounds. On Lake Fanny Hooe. Copper Harbor. 80 campsites. Sand beach, laundromat, sauna. 906/289-4451.

INFORMATION:
Copper Country Chamber of Commerce. Shelden Avenue and Portage Street, Houghton, Michigan 49931. 906/482-5240.
Calumet-Laurium-Keweenaw Chamber of Commerce. P.O. Box 167, Calumet, Michigan 49931. 906/337-4579.

LODGING:
Chippewa Motel and Restaurant. On Portage Lake, 7 miles south of Houghton on U.S. 41. 906/523-7716.
Arcadian Acres Motel. U.S. 41 in Calumet. 906/482-0228.
Copper Harbor: Bella Vista Motel and Cottages. May 15-October 15. 906/289-4213.
Lake Fanny Hooe Resort. On Lake Fanny Hooe near Fort Wilkins State Park. 906/289-4451.
Copper Crown Motel. 235 Hancock, Hancock. 906/482-6111.

Houghton to Copper Harbor Map

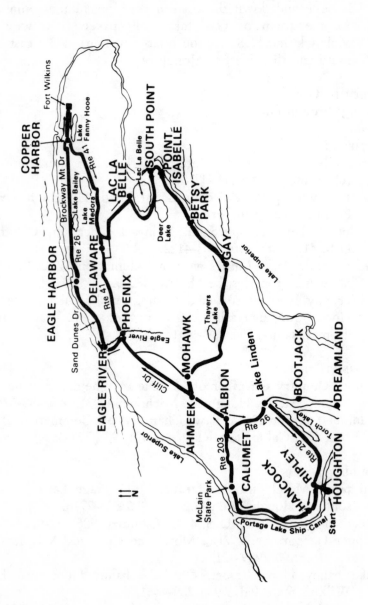

RESTAURANTS:
Douglass House in Houghton. 517 Shelden Avenue (U. S. 41).
   100-year-old setting. 7-1:30 p.m., 5-8:30 p.m. Closed
   holidays. 906/482-5000.
Finlandia Restaurant and Bakery. 211 Quincy, Hancock.
   906/482-3981.
Marja's Dairy Kreeme. M-26 in Laurium. 906/337-1205.
Skufca Restaurant. 427 Fifth St., Calumet. 906/337-9808.
Scandinavian House. 333 Hecla St., Laurium. 906/337-9874.

BIKE CARE:
Hancock Bike Shop. Hancock. 906/482-5234.

TRANSPORTATION:
Air service to Houghton. Bus to Houghton. No trains.

CRYSTAL LAKE TO INTERLOCHEN

   This truly wilderness experience is for a biker who doesn't
mind hilly terrain. The scenic countryside is dotted with ice-
blue lakes, cherry orchards, and sand dunes that sometimes
look like another planet. You pass no less than 13 lakes on this
trip which runs along river and stream beds. The beautiful
scenery and three long, downhill runs make up for the several
quite difficult hills.
   One of the attractions in the area is the Point Betsie
Lighthouse located just north of Frankfort. Built before the
Civil War, it is one of the oldest lighthouses still in operation
on the Great Lakes, and is a favorite subject for artists and
photographers.
   In July, the Grand Traverse region has a National Cherry
Festival to celebrate its cherry harvest each year. Parades,
water sports, exhibits, and concerts are just a few of the
activities in the summer. In spring, this same area is abloom
with blossoms in the many orchards.
   Some of the best swimming in Lake Michigan is along this
shoreline. Inland, you'll pass forest lawns covered with wildflowers, and, at night, hear the lonely music of the loons on
small lakes.

The Platte River Anadromous Fish Hatchery is one of the largest and most modern hatcheries in the world. It has a visitor center and tours can be arranged.

In the fall the hardwood forests are ignited by early frosts, and burst into color.

By continuing up Airport Road, you can reach Sleeping Bear Dunes North Unit, which has fine scenery for photographers. Dune rides are available near the North Park Unit.

At Interlochen State Park, you can camp, swim and fish. Be sure to visit the world-famous Interlochen National Music Camp, which has a regular schedule of concerts and performances throughout the year. The beautiful campus is located in a virgin pine forest bordering Green and Duck lakes. In summer, 1,500 students from all over the U.S. gather at the camp from late June to mid-August to study music, dance, and drama. Visitors can watch the daily concerts, plays, recitals and other presentations. Nearby, Interlochen State Park on Duck Lake provides 550 campsites set in virgin pine.

If you go in early fall, remember that the further north you go, the cooler it will be. Be prepared for some chilly nights along with that gorgeous harvest moon.

Fifteen miles northeast of the Interlochen campus is Traverse City, center of the cherry industry. An enormous flock of mute swans, numbering over 700, make their winter and spring home near Traverse Bay. During the summer, these beautiful creatures scatter in pairs throughout the area.

As you ride along the Lake Michigan shoreline, you'll pass shifting hills of sand covered with bracken fern and tiny, stunted trees. Sometimes these sand dunes pile as high as 600 feet.

LOCATION:
Lower Peninsula, northwest Michigan in Benzie, Lelanau and Grand Traverse counties.

TERRAIN:
Hilly, with some difficult climbs.

TRAVEL:
About 160 miles.

TIME:
5 days.

ROAD SURFACE:
Paved.

TYPE OF TRIP:
Tour or camp.

ROUTE:
Begin in Frankfort. Go west from Frankfort for best and safest use of hills. Otherwise there is a dangerous stop at the corner of Warren and Crystal Drive. Take M22 west and south around Betsie Lake to River Road, east (Benzonia) ¼ mile north (Careful! You must stop in the middle of a steep hill) to 31, 2 miles north (Beulah) to Crystal Drive, west 2½ miles (Warren), north to Platte Road, northwest to 22, north to Deadstream Road, southeast (Honor) to B1, east to Goose Road, southeast to 31 (forest campground here), east 2 miles (Platte River Anadromous Fish Hatchery) to Thompsonville Road, south 2½ miles to Cinder Road, east 5 miles to Bendon Road (jog south over tracks) to Rhodes Road, east to Diamond Park Road, east to 137, 1 mile south to Interlochen State Park (camping). Take 137 north to South Long Lake Road, north to West Long Lake Road, north 5 miles to 610, west to (Lake Ann Village) Almira, west 4½ miles to Royle Road which joins Fowler Road, west to Indian Hill Road (671), south to Deadstream Road (673) to Benzie State Park, then northwest to 122, west to Sutter Road, west to 22, south to Frankfort.

WHEN TO GO:
Spring through fall.

CAMPING:

Interlochen State Park. 550 sites. Showers, swimming, refreshments.

Frankfort. Betsie River Campgrounds. One mile south on Hwy 22 from Jct 115 and 22, then 1 mile east on River Road. 85 sites. Showers. May 1–November 1.

Mud Lake Campground near Interlochen. One mile east on 31 then 2 miles north on Wildwood Road.

Rustic Haven Campground near Interlochen. One mile north on 137, ½ mile east on 31, then ¼ mile north on Rogers Road. 26 sites.

Lake Ann Campgrounds. 3 miles west on 610, then 1 mile south on Reynolds Road. 26 sites.

Near Honor: Sleeping Bear Dunes Campground. 5 miles west on Deadstream Road, then ½ mile south on 22. 83 sites. Laundry, store, showers. April 15–October 31.

INFORMATION:

Frankfort Chamber of Commerce, Box 566, 49635. 616/352-4601.

Traverse City, Box 387, 49684. 616/947-5075.

LODGING:

In Beulah, Rosier's. One mile south of Benzonia on 31. 616/882-4891.

Sou'wester Motel. Frankfort. 26 units. 616/352-9614.

Starlite Motel. Interlochen. Midway between Interlochen and Honor on U.S. 31. 12 units. 616/275-7383.

RESTAURANTS:

Frankfort. Faught's Wharfside. 300 Main Street. 3 blocks west of 22. 616/352-7691.

Money's Fine Foods in Honor. On U.S. 31 near Platte River. 616/325-3255.

Crystal Lake to Interlochen Map

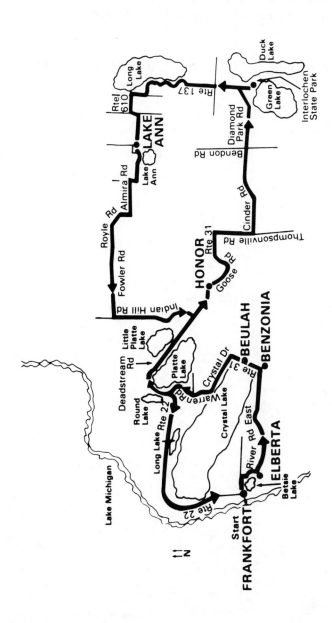

BIKE CARE:
Neil's Wheels in Beulah. 270 Benzie Road. 616/882–4911.
Suttons' Bay Touring Company in Glen Arbor. 616/334–3805.

TRANSPORTATION:
Air service to Fling and Traverse City. Bus to Traverse City
and Frankfort.

9

Minnesota: Introduction and Trails

State Capital: St. Paul
State Flower: Pink and White Lady's Slipper
State Tree: Red Pine
State Bird: Loon
State Nickname: "North Star State"

It's cold up there! Sure it is, but it's also a natural wilderness, with forests, lakes, and a good variety of wildlife. And though temperatures of well below freezing are standard winter fare, the summer climate is perfect biking weather. It's not too hot or humid, with July temperatures ranging in the 60s or 70s. Just bring warm clothing, plan your trip in the summer months, when the temperatures at International Falls do reach into the 80s, and be prepared to be self-sufficient. Bring insect repellent spring through fall. Mosquitos, sometimes called the Minnesota state bird, are enormous and plentiful.

On a bike, you can get a close-up view of Minnesota's beautiful wildflowers.

Bikecentennial, of the U.S. Forest Service, hopes to develop a network of long-distance trails connecting many parts of the U.S. by using the Trans America Bike Trail, which runs from Virginia to Oregon, as a backbone.

One route being researched is the Great River Route, which runs parallel to the Mississippi River from its source in northern Minnesota near Lake Itasca, to the Louisiana Delta. This route is a challenging and scenic trip for a biker who has several weeks to spend cycling.

In Minnesota, wildlife ranging from turtles, grey squirrels, and ruffled grouse, to deer, foxes, black bear, and moose are common. You won't see any wolves, as they prefer to keep away from their predators, but this endangered species also roams the Minnesota forests.

In addition to its unspoiled wilderness and Lake Superior shoreline, Minnesota offers plays, orchestras, and opera in the metropolitan Minneapolis-St. Paul area, and many historic places that make good biking targets.

Split Rock Lighthouse is a reminder of the past, with its two-audio-tone compressed-air fog signal, and derrick and oil house which were used to load station supplies up to the lighthouse until 1916.

Visit Indian museums, forts, historic homes (such as that of Charles Lindbergh), see petroglyphs, which are ancient carvings on red rock and date back as far as 3,000 B.C., or stop at Pelican Rapids, where two 12,000-year-old human skeletons that were found indicate man lived in the area long ago. The Minnesota Historical Society is a nationally acclaimed leader in state and local history, and operates 19 major historic sites, and hundreds of historical points of interest throughout the state. For brochures write:

> The Minnesota Historical Society
> Fort Snelling Branch
> Building 25
> St. Paul, Minnesota 55111
> Phone: 612/726-1171

Minnesota, whose name comes from the Sioux Indian word meaning "Sky-colored Water," reaches farther north than any state except Alaska. The landscape has many beautiful features for the seasoned biker to enjoy, such as wilderness, rolling prairies, fertile valleys, high bluffs, rocky shorelines, long ridges, and thousands of lakes. About half the population lives in and around Minneapolis-St. Paul and Duluth, which is the state's third largest city and a great iron ore shipping port.

Voyageurs National Park in the northeast part of the state is America's newest National Park. The Boundary Waters Canoe Area, which is federally protected as a wilderness preserve, is also in northeastern Minnesota. This area is largely roadless and traveled mainly by canoe. Bike into this forest along the Lake Superior shoreline, or on the few county roads, most of which are unpaved.

As early as 1840, Minnesota was a vacationland and health resort, for it has approximately one square mile of water for every 20 miles of land, and over 14,000 inland lakes.

Middle northern Minnesota is a resort location. The towns of Bemidji and Brainerd are two of the state's largest vacation centers.

In the southwest corner near Pipestone, the famous pipestone quarries were used by the Indians to make peace pipes. Today Indians in the state number 11,000, mostly Chippewas, many of them living on reservations.

Along the St. Croix and Mississippi rivers, the high bluffs offer panoramic views of the countryside.

Because tourism is an important industry, you can get helpful information when planning a bike tour. For hotel and motel information, write:

> Minnesota Hotel and Motor Hotel Association
> 2001 University
> St. Paul, Minnesota 55104
> Phone: 612/647-0107

For restaurants:

> Minnesota Restaurant Association
> 2001 University
> St. Paul, Minnesota 55104
> Phone: 612/647-0107

For campgrounds:

> Minnesota Association of Campground Operators
> P. O. Box 22499
> Robbinsdale, Minnesota 55422

For highway maps and information:

> Minnesota Highway Department

Highway Building
St. Paul, Minnesota 55155
Phone: 612/296-3581

Minnesota is divided into six vacation areas. For information on each of these areas write the following addresses:
Northeast:

Minnesota Arrowhead Association
Hotel Duluth
Duluth, Minnesota 55802
Phone: 218/722-0874

Middle Northern:

Heartland
P.O. Box 442
Brainerd, Minnesota 56401
Phone: 218/829-1615

Southeast:

Hiawathaland
212 First Avenue, S.W.
Rochester, Minnesota 55901
Phone: 507/288-8970

Surrounding Minneapolis-St. Paul:

Metroland
c/o Northern Dakota County Chamber of
    Commerce
Suite 101
33 East Wentworth
West St. Paul, Minnesota 55118
Phone: 612/222-5889

Southwest:

> Pioneerland
> Box 999
> Manka, Minnesota 56001
> Phone: 507/345-4517

Northwest:

> Vikingland USA
> Box 545
> Battle Lake, Minnesota 56515
> Phone: 218/864-8181

For other information on Minnesota write:

> Minnesota Tourist Information Center
> 480 Cedar St.
> St. Paul, Minnesota 55101
> Phone: 612/296-5029

For County Maps, write:

> Minnesota Department of Highways
> Room B-20
> St. Paul, Minnesota 55155

For other bike trails in Minnesota write:

> Minnesota Council of American Youth Hostels, Inc.
> 475 Cedar Street
> St. Paul, Minnesota 55101
> Phone: 612/222-0771, Extension 368.

MINNESOTA BIKE RULES

Obey all traffic laws and ride as near to the right hand shoulder of the road as is practical. Exercise care when passing a standing vehicle or one moving in the same direction. Don't ride more than two abreast, except on bike paths. Where usable bike paths are provided, you must use them and not the road. Don't ride your bike on the sidewalk in a business district. Your bike must have a light at night that can be seen 500 feet ahead, and a red reflector. No bike can be ridden by more persons than it was designed for (that is, no passengers!).

MISSISSIPPI RIVER RED WING TO WABASHA TRIP

The town of Cannon Falls is tucked in a nook of the lovely Cannon River valley. As a change of pace from biking, leave your cycles at Red Wing, and canoe or inner tube the Cannon River from Cannon Falls to Red Wing. Use a car shuttle to get to Cannon Falls. (See Chapter 4.)

Overlooks on the route in Red Wing give marvelous panoramas of the Hiawatha Valley. You can enjoy the setting from Memorial Skyline Drive, or from an excursion boat trip along the Mississippi. Several examples of 19th century architecture, such as the Sheldon Mansion, which has been restored, can be seen in town. The mansion has shops and a tea room.

If you bike along the Mississippi to Frontenac Station, you can explore old Frontenac on county road 2, where homes built in the late 1850s face the river. The Episcopal Church here has been holding Sunday services for 100 years. At Frontenac State Park there is a fine view of Lake Pepin, and camping and hiking areas.

Majestic bluffs rise in grandeur along the western bank of the Mississippi River on this gem of a biking trip.

Lake City, on the shore of Lake Pepin, is the place where waterskiing was invented by Ralph Samuelson in 1922.

Further south along the river highway is Read's landing, where the county museum is housed in a brick schoolroom.

Wabasha, named for the Dakota Sioux chiefs whose villages were in the region, was once a steamboat river commerce port. Wabasha has Minnesota's oldest hotel, the Anderson

House, built in 1856. Here you can stay in antique-furnished rooms, and eat Pennsylvania Dutch cuisine.

All but a small part of this invigorating ride is in the Memorial Hardwood State Forest.

LOCATION:
Southeastern Minnesota, Goodhue and Wabasha counties.

TERRAIN:
Hilly.

TRAVEL:
125 miles.

TIME:
2-3 days.

ROAD SURFACE:
Paved, and 3 miles gravel.

TYPE OF TRIP:
Day, tour, or camp.

ROUTE:
Begin at Cannon Falls. Take route 19 east to 61, southeast into Red Wing. Follow 61 south along the Mississippi River to Wabasha. Take 60 southwest to Zumbro Falls. Take 60 three miles past Zumbro Falls to county road 7 (part gravel), north to Bellechester, to CR 2, north to intersection of CR 9. Take 9 west past Goodhue to 6, north to 10, northeast into Red Wing. At Red Wing take 61 back northwest to 19, south to Cannon Falls.

WHEN TO GO:
Spring through fall.

CAMPING:
Cannon Falls KOA. 1½ miles east on 19. 100 sites. Showers, laundry, store. April 15-November 15.

Mississippi River, Red Wing to Wabasha Map

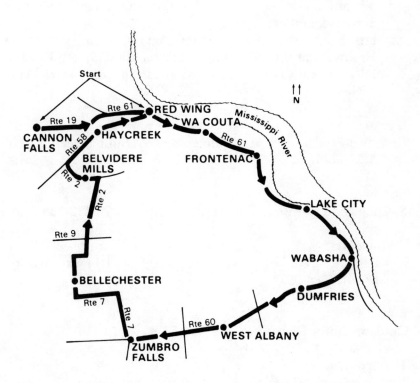

Frontenac State Park in Lake City. 5 miles northwest on U.S. 61. 56 sites. Showers. May–October 1.

Big Sioux Campgrounds in Wabasha. 812 Pembroke. 22 sites. Showers.

Pioneer Campground in Wabasha. 4½ miles south on U.S. 61. 5½ miles east on Pioneer Trail, follow signs. 150 sites. Showers, laundry, store.

Zumbro Falls. Bluff Valley Campgrounds. 2 miles west on Highway 60 then 1½ miles south on Bluff Valley Road (a hilly, narrow access road). 81 sites. Showers, store. May 1–November 1.

INFORMATION:
Red Wing Chamber of Commerce, 416 Bush Street, 55066. 612/388-4719.

LODGING:
Sterling Motel in Red Wing, 1½ mile east on 61. 612/388-3568.

RESTAURANTS:
Nybo's Restaurant, Red Wing. 328 Main St. 1 block north of 63. 612/388-3597.

BIKE CARE:
Outdoor Store, Red Wing. 612/388-5358.

TRANSPORTATION:
Train through Wabasha to Red Wing. Bus through Wabasha to Red Wing. Air service to Rochester, Minnesota.

LAKE ITASCA AND THE MISSISSIPPI HEADWATERS

If you ever wondered where all that water in the Mississippi River began, you'll find out on this trip in northern Minnesota. You circle quiet lakes in the Mississippi watershed, cut through dense forests, and muscle, or walk, your bike up, and then soar down, wooded foothills. You might hear the

Minnesota's forests can seem almost endless, when seen by bike.

lonely cry of the loon, or the eerie wail of a wolf on a silent evening as you warm yourself by the campfire, if you are lucky. The biking is rugged, but the rewards are great, as you immerse yourself in the clean air, crisp weather, and changing contours of the land.

Located in between the resort towns of Brainerd and Bemidji, this route is in the rolling hills and valleys of Minnesota's forest and lake region. The further north or east you ride, the more these hills resemble mountains. Lakes in the area are known for their clear water and sandy beaches.

The headwaters of the Mississippi are located at Lake Itasca, where you can walk across the narrow, ankle-deep stream of transparent water, or drop a twig in it, and imagine it traveling all the way to New Orleans. From Lake Itasca, the Mississippi River meanders 2,200 miles to the Gulf of Mexico.

The history of Lake Itasca includes Indians, voyageurs, lumberjacks, and hardy pioneers.

An interpretive center has information on nearby Indian burial mounds. Thursday through Sunday in the summer, local residents give craft demonstrations and sell their handicrafts in the park. Also nearby is a log cabin, built in 1893.

The world's largest Norway Pine grows near Nicollet Creek on the west arm of Lake Itasca. It has a 115-inch circumference and has survived at least six different forest fires.

Park Rapids, originally a lumbering town, is a popular resort area, even though lumbering is still important. Fish Hook Lake, in the city, has some of the best fishing waters in the country. At the Aqua Park Rapids Aquarium, more than 100 native fish are on view. Deertown is a frontier village with stagecoach rides and tame deer.

On this trip you ride through Paul Bunyan State Forest, Huntersville State Forest, Foothills State Forest, and Badoura State Forest.

LOCATION:
Middle northern Minnesota in Clearwater, Hubbard, Wadena, and Cass counties.

TERRAIN:
Hilly.

TRAVEL:
About 150 miles.

TIME:
4 days.

ROAD SURFACE:
Paved. Gravel side roads in the area.

TYPE OF TRIP:
Tour or camp.

ROUTE:

Begin at Lake Itasca. Take 200/71 south and then east to Lake George to 4, south to Park Rapids to 34, east to 11, south to 87, east to 13, south to Huntersville to 18, east and south (becomes 27) to 27, south to 12, east and north to 64, north through Chamberlain and Akeley, 16 miles past Akeley take 200 west to Lake Itasca.

WHEN TO GO:

Summer and fall.

CAMPING:

Staves Resort in Lake Itasca. In town. 45 sites. Showers, store.

Breeze Campgrounds in Park Rapids. 9 miles north on 71. 144 sites. Showers, laundry, store, swimming pool. May 12–October 1.

Itasca State Park. 28 miles north on 71. 237 sites. Showers.

Big Pines in Park Rapids. ¾ mile east on 34 then ½ mile south on Central Avenue. 70 sites. Showers.

Pine Mountain Manor in Backus. 2½ miles southwest on 87. 50 sites.

Spring Bay Farm Campground at Akeley. 2 miles east on 34, then 2 miles north on access road. 20 sites. Showers, pit toilets.

Camper's Paradise in Nevis. 3 miles west on Belle Taine Road, follow signs. 80 sites. Showers. Memorial Day to Labor Day.

Stony Point Campground in the Chippewa National Forest near Walker. 6 miles southeast on 26/371/200. Four miles north on 13. 2 miles east on access road. 45 sites. June 1–October 1.

Bayview Resort and Campgrounds near Walker. 3 miles north on 371. 77 sites. Showers, laundry, store. May 14 to October 14.

Silver Springs Resort near Walker. 3 miles north on 371. Northwest on Kabekona Bay Road. 14 sites. May 15–October 11.

Lake Itasca and the Mississippi Headwaters Map

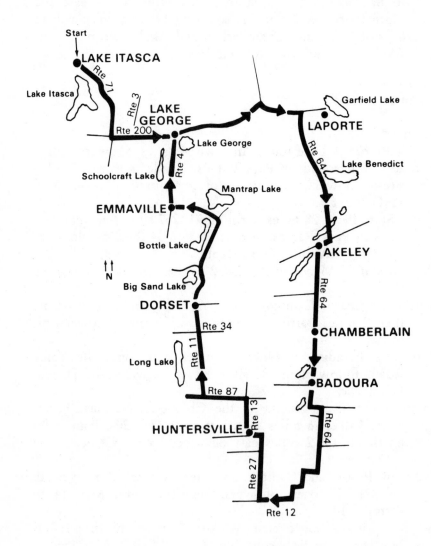

INFORMATION:
Bemidji Area Chamber of Commerce, Box 806, 56601.
218/751-3540.

LODGING:
Lake Itasca State Park. Douglas Lodge. Lake Itasca.
Northern Pine Lodge, Park Rapids. 7 miles north on 71. 2
miles east. 218/723-5103.
Peterson's Northwood Beach in Walker. 1 block north of 371.
218/547-1702.

RESTAURANTS:
Alpine Dining Room, Park Rapids. 218/266-3306.
Places to eat in resort towns on the road.
Antlers in Park Rapids. 600 North Park Avenue.
Rapid River Logging Camp. 5 miles north on Lake George
Road.

BIKE CARE:
Gambles. 218/732-4443. Park Rapids.

TRANSPORTATION:
Train to Staples (20 miles south and east of Nimrod). Bus to
Bemidji. Air service to Bemidji (30 miles northeast of
Lake Itasca).

NORTH SHORE OF LAKE SUPERIOR TO CANADA

There's a quip around Duluth that says summer was on a
Tuesday last year. It's just a joke, but be prepared for cool
weather on this trip along the gorgeous, rugged coastline of
Lake Superior, north of Duluth. July temperatures in northern
Minnesota average in the 60's and 70's, so bring warm
clothing. A hearty biker can ride along the shoreline from
Duluth to Grand Portage, a distance of over 150 miles one
way. The scenery is spectacular, but as this is the only
highway in the area, all types of vehicles travel on it. Watch
out for trucks and RV's, which can blow you off the road if
they are traveling fast.

Even though there are campgrounds, resorts, and small towns about every twenty miles, be largely self-sufficient, and plan your meals in advance. Biking in cooler weather, you will burn more energy and eat more than you ordinarily do.

Carry an extra brake cable, brake pads, and other equipment so that your trip isn't spoiled if you have bike trouble. There is bus service between Grand Portage and Duluth. You can either make this a round trip of a total of 300 miles, or take the bus back to Duluth. Find out in advance what the current requirements are for shipping bikes as baggage on a bus.

This trip can also be a leg of a journey around Lake Superior. If you are an experienced cyclist and love the shoreline, the trip should take between two and three weeks. Once you get into Canada, the old shoreline highway criss-crosses the new Trans-Canadian Highway. Though the old highway is overgrown with grasses in places, it is unused by cars, and yet is, as of this writing, still traversable by bike.

Begin your trip at the town of French River, north of Duluth, on route 61, and ride north through Two Harbors. You will stay on route 61 all the way up to Grand Portage.

You pass through many-leveled Gooseberry Falls, and listen to the crash of breakers on Minnesota's craggy shoreline at historic Split Rock Lighthouse.

Iron ore boats load at Two Harbors, Silver Bay, and Taconite Harbor.

At Grand Marais, take county road 12 into the Boundary Waters Canoe Area, if you feel like getting a change from the shoreline scenery.

LOCATION:
Northeastern Minnesota, in St. Louis, Lake, and Cook counties.

TERRAIN:
Hilly.

TRAVEL:
About 150 miles one way.

TIME:
4 days one way.

ROAD SURFACE:
Paved on 61.

TYPE OF TRIP:
Tour or camp.

ROUTE:
Begin at French River, north of Duluth on Route 61. Take 61 all the way up to the Grand Portage Indian Reservation. Return by bus to Duluth or allow double your time, and retrace 61 back to French River.

WHEN TO GO:
Summer.

CAMPING:
Duluth Tent and Trailer Camp. 8 miles northeast on scenic 61. 53 sites. Shower, laundry. May 1–October 15.

Linden's Cabins and Camping in Two Harbors. Store, shower. On 61. Box 93, Two Harbors, Minnesota 55616. 218/834-3796.

Lamb's Campground in Schroeder. 55613. 218/663-7292. 70 sites. Showers, sauna, laundry, store. May 20 to October 31. 80 miles northeast of Duluth on 61.

Grand Marais Cascade River State Park. 10 miles south on 61. 45 sites. Primitive. April 1–October 1.

Hollow Rock Resort in Grand Portage. 12 miles east on 61. 24 sites. Showers, store. April 15 to November 15.

Helen's Campground in Knife River. In town on 61. 30 sites. Showers. April 1 to October 31.

Gooseberry Falls State Park. 13 miles north of Two Harbors on 61. 125 sites. Showers, laundry. May 15 to October 15.

Scenic Point Resort. 1 mile northeast of Two Harbors on 61 then ¼ mile on Lakeshore. 40 sites. Showers, lake swimming. May 1–October 20.

Temperance River State Park. 1 mile north of Schroeder on 61. 26 sites. Showers.

Grand Marais Tourist Park in town on 61. 56 sites. Showers, lake swimming.

INFORMATION:

Duluth Chamber of Commerce, 325 Harbor Drive, Duluth 55802.

Grand Portage National Monument, Box 666, Grand Marais 55604. 218/387-2788.

LODGING:

Two Harbors Motel, Box 404, ½ mile southwest on 61. 218/834-5171.

Duluth Hotel, 231 East Superior Street (U.S. 61). 218/727-4577.

Two Harbors Motel. On U.S. 61. 218/834-4048.

RESTAURANTS:

Chinese Lantern, 403 West Superior, Duluth. 218/722-7481.

BIKE CARE:

Twin Ports Cyclery, Duluth. 218/727-3479.

Stewart Wheel Goods, Duluth. 218/724-5101.

University Sports, Duluth. 218/728-1548.

TRANSPORTATION:

Bus between Duluth and Grand Portage. Air service to Duluth. Train service to Duluth.

North Shore of Lake Superior to Canada Map

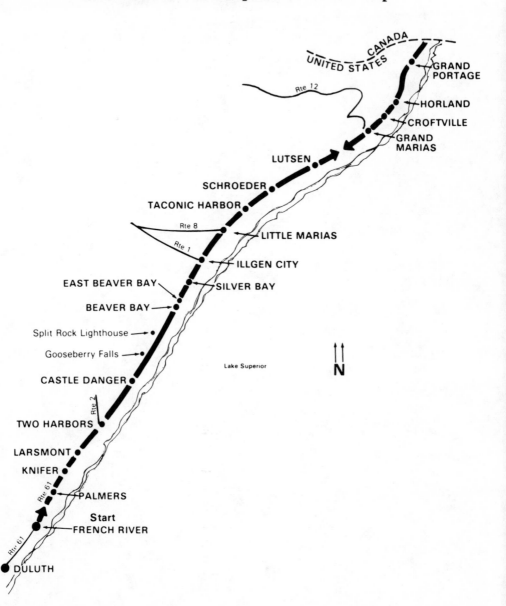

10

Wisconsin: Introduction and Trails

State Capital: Madison
State Flower: Wood Violet
State Tree: White Pine
State Bird: Robin
State Nickname: "Badger State"

Bring your bicycle, and you'll find a place that's scenic and restful almost anywhere in this state. Known worldwide as "America's Dairyland," the tempo of life in Wisconsin is as peaceful as the Guernsey and Holstein cows you see grazing in the pastures. But there is more to the biking terrain than just plains.

The ragged Wisconsin boundary follows natural water courses for most of its length, and frames large areas of plains, small, stream-cut plateaus, and many erosion-worn mountains. Generally, the elevation in the north is higher than the south, with the lowest elevation of 581 feet occurring along the Lake

Many of Wisconsin's well-known bikeways are converted railroad beds and trestles, such as this section near New Glarus.

Michigan shoreline, and the highest elevation of 1,940 feet at Rib Mountain, near Wausau. The state has nearly 9,000 interior lakes, the majority of which are located in the north. Rolling hill and pasture surround flat cranberry marshes in the middle of the state.

In the late 19th century, lumbering companies exploited the virgin forests which once covered most of the state, and left raw gashes of burnt and cut tree stumps. By the 1920s, however, a strong conservation program was in effect and the state reforested. Virtually all the woods you ride through now are second-growth trees.

For the biker, this strong conservation attitude is good news. Bikers, who don't contribute to the pollution revolution, are welcomed, and many bike clubs promote the development of good roads and bikeways. For information on Wisconsin Bike Clubs write:

The League of American Wheelmen
19 South Bothwell
Palatine, Illinois 60067

Wisconsin has over 18,000 miles of excellent paved secondary roads.

There are five major geographical areas to bike through in this state. The first is the western uplands area, which has the highest altitude, and includes the Galena-Black River Ridge, the Baraboo Ridge, and many other regions of natural beauty. Biking here is for the more experienced cyclist.

The eastern ridges and lowlands area is a glaciated plain running roughly from the Menominee River and Door County south. Fertile soil and level topography make for easy biking through farm country.

Between the western uplands and the eastern ridges and lowlands is a flat expanse of sandy landscape broken frequently by buttes and mesas such as those at the Wisconsin Dells, Camp Douglas, and Black River Falls. This central plain, as it is called, makes for generally pleasant family biking with some low, rounded hills and moraines to add a bit of challenge.

Except for a small plain touching on Lake Superior, which is called the Lake Superior lowland, the rest of the state is in the northern highland. This plain, with its moderate terrain and underlying pre-cambrian rock, is evidence that Wisconsin was at one time a lofty mountain range. Biking here is idyllic. Rivers in the area have many rapids and waterfalls, and biking through the forests is at once invigorating and calming.

The northern section of the state is more rugged, has fewer civilized concessions for the biker such as restaurants and motels, but offers lovely natural sights. It's not uncommon to see white-tail deer, the Wisconsin state wildlife animal, grazing in the twilight here, and the northern skies offer a special kind of night light. A spectacular display, the aurora borealis, which is correlated with sunspot activity, can often be seen in the northern portion of the state. One of the most beautiful sights in the heavens, it occurs 60 to 680 miles above the earth.

There are also plenty of down-to-earth activities as well. Wisconsin county fairs in July and August are as plentiful as fireflies in June. LaCrosse, the Square Dancing Capital of the

World, holds a mammoth Spring Fling each year, and in June, the Heidi Festival in New Glarus reflects that city's Swiss heritage. The World Lumberjack Championship of logrolling, rigging, chopping, climbing, and sawing brings the legend of Paul Bunyan to life in the northern town of Haywood in July.

To this land, Swedes, Poles, Swiss, Germans, Danes, and Finns brought their pioneer heritage and gave the state its uniquely American flavor. You can absorb the culture of these peoples in their festivals, museums, parades, and historic areas.

The population of Wisconsin is most concentrated in the southeastern portion of the state. As you fan out north and west, it becomes progressively more sparse. In the Kenosha area, there are about 90 persons per square mile; near the Apostle Islands on the Lake Superior shoreline, this number is between 2 and 18.

North of the city of Horicon, in Dodge and Fond du Lac counties, the Horicon Marsh Wildlife Area is a refuge for migrating waterfowl. It is a combination of open water, productive marsh, and dry areas. In recent years, the peak population of migrating birds has risen to as many as 147,000 geese. Migration periods last from February through March, and from late September through November. The land is level here, and the best way to appreciate the multitude of waterfowl in the area is by bike. However, many autos filled with tourists who also come to see the geese are on the road at this time, so bike during the week, rather than on the weekend, if you can.

Although hunting is allowed in season near this area, the booming sounds you may hear as you ride are not necessarily from guns. Farmers in the area attempt to keep the migrating waterfowl off of their lands by setting off periodic explosions. A solid blanket of geese covers the land, and the problem of too many waterfowl is one the federal government is working to solve.

One nickname for Wisconsin is "Badger State." It comes from the early lead miners who lived in holes dug into the hillside, which resembled the homes of the badger.

Almost two million cows in the state produce enough milk

a year for 30 million people, and enough cheese for 79 million people. Crops of beets, corn, cranberries, and potatoes are harvested in various parts of the state.

In addition to good county trunk roads, this state has several designated bike trails.

The East-West Wisconsin Bikeway, a 300-mile trail that crosses the entire state from LaCrosse to Kenosha, is probably the best known trail in the nation. Write for a map-brochure, *The Wisconsin Bikeway,* to:

> The Wisconsin Bikeway
> Department of Natural Resources
> Box 450
> Department B
> Madison, Wisconsin 53701

The brochure gives state camping facilities and bike shops along the route, as well as monthly rainfall, temperature averages, and prevailing winds.

A moderate trail-user fee is collected on portions of the East-West bikeway that was once a railroad bed. This fee is charged those 18 years of age or older, who bike the trail from April 1 to the Saturday nearest October 27. There is a toll on the 32-mile Elroy-Sparta section, the Sugar River, Ahnapee, and Bearskin State Trail portions of the Bikeway. Many towns along the more popular sections of the trail have shops that rent all types of bikes, from balloon tire, tandems, and three-speeds with child carriers, to 10-speeds.

Thirteen counties have self-guided excursion tours of the East-West Bikeway, featuring the Ice Age Bicycle Trail. These counties are Dane, Green, Juneau, Columbia, LaCrosse, Marquette, Monroe, Racine, Rock, Sauk, Walworth, Waushara, and Waukesha counties. For brochures write:

> Wisconsin Division of Tourism
> P. O. Box 7606
> Madison, Wisconsin 53707

You can also get a schedule of bus, air, and train routes in Wisconsin, and information on historical places of interest, from the Division of Tourism.

County highway maps (8½ by 11 inches) are available for a small fee by writing:

> Document Sales
> Wisconsin Department of Transportation
> P.O. Box 7426
> Madison, Wisconsin 53707

Topographic maps are available from:

> Wisconsin Geological and Natural History Survey
> 1815 University Avenue
> Madison, Wisconsin 53706

The city of Milwaukee has a designated, scenic 75-mile bike route. Write for the Milwaukee County Bike Tour Map to:

> Greater Milwaukee Convention and Visitor's Bureau
> 828 North Broadway
> Milwaukee, Wisconsin 53202

The cities of Oshkosh, Madison, Eau Claire, and Wisconsin Dells have designated certain streets and highways as bikeways. For more information, write to their respective chambers of commerce.

In addition to the East-West Bikeway and city bikeways, a North-South Bikeway extending the length of the state has been completed. On it you can travel 325 miles from LaCrosse to Bayfield and the Apostle Islands in Lake Superior. For a pamphlet on the North-South Bikeway, write to the Wisconsin Division of Tourism, at the address given above.

Wisconsin has 10 regional tourist councils. For the address of the region you are interested in write:

Vacation and Travel Service
Department of Natural Resources
Box 450
Madison, Wisconsin 53701

Ten bike routes and trails located in Green County, with lengths of between 3.5 and 23 miles can be obtained by writing:

Alpine Trails
Green County Clerk
Monroe, Wisconsin 53566

WISCONSIN BIKE RULES

Ride with traffic, within three feet of the shoulder of the road unless making a turn. Obey all traffic signals, and ride single file on roads with a centerline. Where provided, use a bike path instead of the road. At night have a light on the front of your bike that is visible from 500 feet, and a red reflector on the rear of the bike.

KETTLE MORAINE SOUTH TRIP

About 15,000 years ago, Wisconsin was in the grip of an ice age. Monstrous glaciers moved down from Canada, covering much of the state. When they receded, they left, among other landmarks, Kettle Moraine South, some 20 miles southwest of Milwaukee, and Kettle Moraine North, about 40 miles northwest of the city. These hilly forests were shaped by two tongues of ice that met. As the ice melted, the pressure, friction and buckling deposited tons of rock, gravel and sand between the tongues, or lobes. The resulting long, sinuous ridge rises as much as 300 feet above the surrounding farmland.

An advantage—or disadvantage, depending upon how you

look at it—of biking through either of the Kettle Moraines, is
that they are long, but not wide. One minute you're in them,
the next you're out. If you have bike trouble this is nice,
because help is always nearby. But if you're looking for
solitude, you'll find the trip back to civilization is a quick one.

Whitewater, where you begin your trip, is a pleasant resort
and college town with several lakes in the area. Bus service,
campgrounds, and plenty of restaurants are found in town. If
you pedal on the State Park Drive between Rice and Whitewater lakes, you'll appreciate the slant of some moraine hills.
Rice Lake is six feet lower than Whitewater Lake, even
though they are only 400 feet apart.

The Janesville stagecoach was once routed through the
village, and the tavern of the time had such regulations as
"No more than five to sleep in one bed," "No dogs allowed
upstairs," "Organ grinders to sleep in the wash house," and
"No razor grinders or tinkers taken in."

The pretty University of Wisconsin-Whitewater campus
was established in 1868, and has an art gallery and other
attractions.

On campus behind Hyer Hall is a historic log cabin, the
first house built in town, in 1836.

A doll and antique collection is on view at the Hamilton
House, 328 West Main Street.

In the town of Eagle, which can be reached from county
road X by taking county road NNN south to NN East, is the
Old World Wisconsin living museum. Located 2 miles east of
Eagle, this outdoor ethnic museum is situated on over 500
acres of land.

Farm and village buildings constructed by immigrants who
came to Wisconsin are restored in authentic settings. Operated
by the State Historical Society, the museum is open June 30 to
October 31, 9–5 daily. Admission.

Other side trips of historical interest can be taken to
Waukesha and New Berlin. From Lawndale Avenue take
XXN north to D east and north to Waukesha. Here a restored
19th century inn and local history exhibits are open to the

Two forms of non-motorized transportation meet up in Wisconsin.

public. Admission. Continue on D into New Berlin to visit the New Berlin Historical Society, by appointment. Admission.

As you pass the town of Waterford, stop for a rest at the Heg Memorial Park, and browse through the Burlington Historical Museum in that town.

By taking a side trip from Potter Road north on route G, you arrive in East Troy, where you can visit the trolley museum. The local symphony and orchestra of this town maintain an active schedule, and you can take in a summer night's concert. You might even see parachute jumpers, who take off and float back down to earth in the area.

If you come during the Labor Day weekend, attend the Walworth County Fair, and enjoy livestock shows, carnival rides, horse races, and entertainers.

This is a two-day trip through the closely bunched, rib-like hills and valleys that make up the Kettle Moraine, and the flat, outwash plains in the area. Extend the trip by biking into

Hales Corner, whose monthly farmer's market gives the quiet town a fair-like atmosphere, or ride into Milwaukee and visit its famous zoo.

LOCATION:
Waukesha, Jefferson, and Walworth counties in southeastern Wisconsin.

TERRAIN:
Flat on the outwash plains; steep hills in the Kettle Moraine.

TRAVEL:
About 100 miles, plus side trips.

TIME:
2–3 days.

TYPE OF TRIP:
Tour or camp.

ROUTE:
Begin in Whitewater. Take S. Wisconsin Street south to Clover Valley Road, south to Mills Road, east to Clover Valley Road, south to Kettle Moraine Drive, east and north to H (to Palmyra) to Zion Road, north to H, east to ZZ, northeast around Ottawa Lake, east to 67, south to X, south and east to E, south to Sugden, east to I, north and east to HHH, south to H, west to Hillendale Drive, south to Henneberry Drive, west to F, south (to Waterford and Burlington). Just before Burlington take Honey Lake Road north to Potter, west (to Vienna) to Potter, west to Schmidt Road to H, north (to Tibbits). Take A west through Millard to P, north to Territorial Road, west to Town Road, north to Kettle Moraine Drive, north and east to Clover Valley Road, north to S. Wisconsin St., north to Whitewater.

WHEN TO GO:
Spring through fall.

CAMPING:
East Troy, Pickerel Lake, Highway 20. West PIC A BOO
   Family Campground. 57 sites. From jct 15 and 20, 2½
   miles west on 20, then ½ mile north on Boon Lake
   Heights Road. May 10–September 30.
Laursen's Campground. Whitewater. 275 sites. Hot showers,
   grocery, laundry. Townline Road, southeast side of
   Whitewater Lake.
Whitewater Lake Campground. Kettle Moraine State Forest.
   On Kettle Moraine Drive. 83 sites. Lake swimming.

INFORMATION:
Walworth County Resource and Tourism Council, Court-
   house, Elkhorn 53121.
Whitewater Chamber of Commerce 53190.

RESTAURANTS:
The Green Shutters. On U. S. 12 at 59 and 89. Whitewater.
Crossroads Supper Club. State 67 and 15. Elkhorn. Reserva-
   tions.
Copper Kettle, 140 W. Main Street. Whitewater. 414/473-
   9890.
Red Lantern, 1128 W. Main, Whitewater. 414/473-3711.

LODGING:
Thomas Motel. Elkhorn. On State 67 and 15. 414/723-2955.
Country Squire Motel. Highway 12, Route 1. Whitewater.
   414/473-3659.
Chapel Hills Lakeside Resort. 414/883-2912. South end of
   Whitewater Lake.
Krahn's Resort. West side of Whitewater Lake, Whitewater.
   414/883-2856.

Kettle Moraine South Map

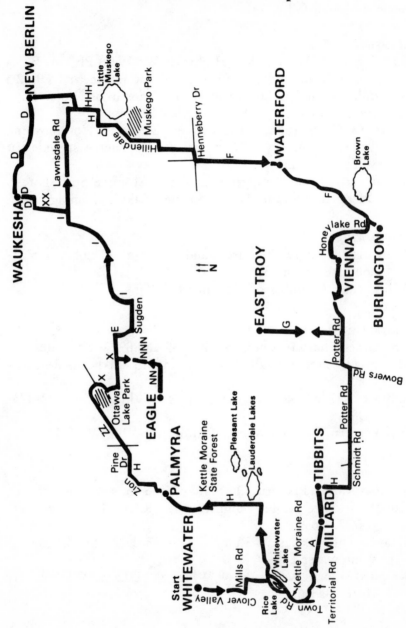

BIKE CARE:
Coast to Coast, 182 Main Street, Whitewater. 414/473-4480.
Roger's Rural Repair, Route 2, Whitewater. 414/495-2484.

TRANSPORTATION:
Bus to Whitewater, Eagle, and Elkhorn. Air service to
  Janesville. Train to Kenosha.

SPRING GREEN TRAIL

Lavish scenery, hills and valleys, winding roads, and unusual historic and cultural landmarks combine to make this trip, located in the unglaciated southwest region of Wisconsin, one of unforgettable charm. Though the trip is a two-to-four-day affair, you can easily spend a week biking in the country surrounding Spring Green. If you wish to take a longer trip, write for the Sauk Trail-Devil's Lake-Dells Area Biking Map to:

> Sauk County
> University Extension Office
> Resource Management Agent
> Box 46
> Baraboo, Wisconsin 53913

The southwest is the only area in Wisconsin that was not covered by the great glacier. It is also the only region where preglacial eras deposited rich veins of lead and tin. Lead attracted the first large group of permanent white settlers to Wisconsin, and mining was the first stable industry in the state.

Nevertheless, the area also has a rich and varied farm region, marshes, bluffs that offer strenuous workouts along the Wisconsin River and long, steep inclines in Baraboo Hills, all of which provide endless biking variety. As you view the broad and peaceful Wisconsin River, you'll find the name, which means "gathering of the waters," apt.

Camp in Reedsburg, where you begin your trip. Leave

early, for the trip to Spring Green is almost 50 miles (more, if
you decide to take the long route from La Valle to Ironton).
In springtime, budding trees and freshly plowed fields stimu-
late the senses on this very hilly trip. Summer brings rich
crops and luxuriant foliage, and in fall, hardwoods changing
color intermingle with rock outcroppings to make each turn in
the road an endlessly refreshing experience. You ride around
Lake Redstone, a man-made lake.

At La Valle, either take a four mile direct route to Ironton,
or follow county road G northwest and then back to Ironton,
adding about 10 miles of hills and panoramas to your trip.

From Ironton, take county road G to Spring Green. The
route follows a high, rolling plateau with magnificent vistas
throughout the 30 mile ride.

Campsites and motels are available at Spring Green. This
town is renowned as the home of late architect, Frank Lloyd
Wright. Be sure to see the unusual architecture of the Bank of
Spring Green, one of the most recent examples of the Wright
school of thought, which is carried on by his followers at
Taliesen. The Spring Green Restaurant, which overlooks the
Wisconsin River, is also designed by the Taliesen Associates.

Across the river from Spring Green is Tower Hill State
Park, with 22 campsites, a picnic area and hiking trail. Once it
was a community called Helena, which was a river port. The
park has a restored shot tower dating back to the 1850s. It
perches 450 feet above the Wyoming Valley and gives a
magnificent view of the Wisconsin countryside. Operations at
the shot tower have been reopened to show visitors how lead
from mines was hauled by horse or ox team to the smelter,
and then processed. Shot for the Indian wars was formed by
dropping hot lead into cool water from the top of the tower.
When the shot tower was active, six men made 5,000 pounds
of shot a day. Only about one eighth to one sixteenth was
perfect, however; the rest had to be remelted.

Visit the Robert Gard Theatre in Spring Green, which
shows live theatre productions, movies, and "Conversations
with Frank Lloyd Wright." The town also has a swimming

pool, tennis courts, restaurants, cheese factories, and gift and antique shops.

Ride 18 miles to Dodgeville, passing by surprising shops and galleries tucked snugly into the hills.

One mile south of Spring Green is Taliesen, which includes the Frank Lloyd Wright home, barn, architectural school, and four-room schoolhouse. (Admission.) Here 30 students learn and practice Wright's philosophy at the Hillside School, which is located in a park-like setting.

Seven miles down the road is the magnificent "House on the Rock." (Admission.) Begun in the 1940s as a retreat for artisan Alex Jordan, it is situated on a 60-foot chimney rock and includes 13 unique rooms, with treasures from all over the world. In it are housed bronze bells, detailed hand-carved wood panels from India, a Chinese wedding chest and other unusual items. The living room has 30-foot windows; there is a three story bookcase, a grotto room, a two story waterfall tumbling from the wall of one room, a deck that affords vistas all the way to Baraboo Bluffs, 30 miles away, a water garden, and flying bridge and gates. Magnificent art accents this house, as well as oriental dolls, delicate ferns and ivies, and great birches that grow through the floors.

Back on the road, stop at the Uplands Art Studio, and then continue on to Governor Dodge State Park. This is the largest park in the state, and has two man-made lakes for swimming and boating, and hundreds of campsites. Concerts, called "Symphonies of the Hills," are presented in the park several times every summer.

At Dodgeville, the southern point of your trip, see a slag furnace built in 1876, or stop for cider at the Fieldhouse Fruit Farm, probably the first commercial orchard in Wisconsin. There are several good outlets for Wisconsin cheese in this area, and some cheese factories offer tours that allow visitors to watch the process of cheese making.

This is the end of the shorter two, or more, day trip. Car shuttle back to Reedsburg. (See Chapter 4.)

For a four or more day trip, stay overnight at Dodgeville,

then retrace your tracks 18 miles back to Spring Green. Head out to Leland, about 25 miles from Spring Green, where you can camp at the foot of the Baraboo Hills. The next day bike through the Baraboo Hills, which has long inclines that can be tiring. Stop often to enjoy the spectacular views, and delight in the good, winding roads and long downhill runs whose steepness is exhilarating. Sandstone buttes are scattered throughout the area. You travel about 50 miles back to Reedsburg.

LOCATION:
Southwestern Wisconsin in Sauk and Iowa counties.

TERRAIN:
Steep hills.

TRAVEL:
60 miles for shortest trip; 80 miles for a more challenging two-day trip; 130 miles for a four-day trip.

TIME:
2–4 days.

ROAD SURFACE:
Paved.

TYPE OF TRIP:
Tour or camp.

ROUTE:
First day, leave your car in Reedsburg. Start early, taking county road K north 3 miles to F, west around Redstone Lake to La Valle. Take either the shortcut to Ironton, or take G northwest to Ironton. Take G to Spring Green, 30 miles south to Highway 23 (to Dodgeville), car shuttle to Reedsburg.

For an extended trip, follow above route to Dodgeville, then: Retrace your tracks on 23, 18 miles to Spring Green to

23, north 22 miles to WC, east to C, north (to Leland) to C, back to jct of C and PF. Take PF north through hills to D, north to Reedsburg.

WHEN TO GO:
Spring through fall.

CAMPING:
Lighthouse Rock Campground. From center of town, 2½ miles on V. 70 sites. Showers, grocery, swimming, hiking. Reedsburg.

Bob's Riverside Camp. One mile south of Spring Green off Madison Street, on river. Canoe rental, refreshments, pizza, beer. 608/588-2826.

Governor Dodge State Park. 266 sites. 15 miles south of Spring Green on Highway 23. Campsites, picnic areas, showers, hiking, swimming, boating.

Spring Valley Trails. 7 miles north of Dodgeville on 23, then 5 miles west on 130 to Spring Valley Road, then left. Year round camping. 608/935-5725.

Tower Hill State Park. 3 miles southeast of Spring Green on 23. Campsites, picnic area, hiking.

INFORMATION:
Spring Green Chamber of Commerce, 53588. 608/588-2042.
Dodgeville Chamber of Commerce, 53533.

LODGING:
Reedsburg Motel, 1133 East Main Street. 6 blocks east on 23. 608/524-2306.
Crestview Motel in Spring Green. 608/588-2222.
Rest Haven Motel, Spring Green. 608/588-2323.
Spring Green Motel, Spring Green. 608/588-2141.
Little Rock Motel, Dodgeville. 608/935-3386.

RESTAURANTS:
Rock's Motel and Supper Club. Highway 23, 1 mile north of Dodgeville.

Spring Green Trail Map

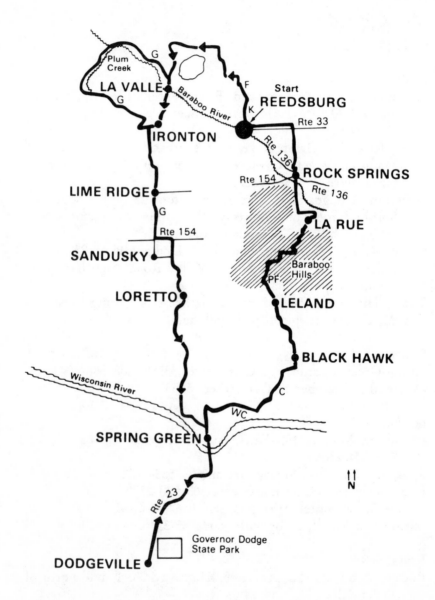

Don-Q-Inn. Route 23, north of Dodgeville.
Dodge Country Drive. Next to Governor Dodge State Park
    on route 23.
Restaurants in Spring Green.

BIKE CARE:
Nemec's Bike Shop. Reedsburg. 608/524-4933.

TRANSPORTATION:
Bus through Dodgeville to Madison, through Spring Green to
    Madison and LaCrosse. Train to Madison and Dubuque,
    Iowa. Air service to Dubuque, Iowa, and Madison.

BARABOO AND THE WISCONSIN DELLS TRIP

Circuses, sandstone cliffs, and easy pedaling make this bike
trip an ideal family outing, but expect to see lots of tourists in
this very popular vacationland. Biking is a good way to see
the area because you aren't harnessed to your car and don't
have to worry about parking.

As this is a busy trip with easy riding and lots of people at
your points of interest, go when you feel sociable, and be sure
to get motel reservations well in advance of your tour.
Confirm them early. Give yourself plenty of time to enjoy the
many sights designed to please both children and adults.

Devil's Lake State Park is the most popular Wisconsin state
park, and is a dramatic example of glacier activity. The
Wisconsin River cut a gorge more than 800 feet deep, then
the melting glacier filled it to make the lake. There are hiking
trails around towering sandstone and sheer quartzite cliffs that
rise 500 feet above the lake on three sides. The park has
swimming, boating, fishing, and camping.

Nearby are Indian mounds and unique geological formations, such as Devil's Doorway, the Needles, Turk's Head, and
Ancient Rock.

Plenty of camping is available all along the trip. By biking
a figure-eight loop, you can start and return to any campsite.
Try for a site at Devil's Lake, as it has the most spectacular

scenery, but arrive early Friday afternoon for a weekend stay, get a site, and spend the rest of the day hiking the trails.

Early the next morning, take county road A north through Baraboo, a town with a rich circus history. It was the birthplace and home of the five Ringling Brothers and the home of their circus until 1918.

Circus World Museum has a fine collection of equipment and costumes, a menagerie of circus animals, and two circus shows daily with acrobats and tight rope walkers, a big top show, a parade, elephant rides, acrobatic German shepherds, and white mules. The 33-acre grounds astride the Baraboo River have the flavor and excitement of a long ago small town circus.

The Von Stiehl Winery on Lynn Street gives 20-minute tours, and samples of the only Montmorency cherry wine in the world.

Ten miles north of Baraboo are the Wisconsin Dells, with their weirdly shaped pinnacles of sandstone rock. Among other souvenirs in town, you can buy Indian moccasins, homemade fudge, and Wisconsin cheese.

Activities abound all summer long at the Wisconsin Dells, from raft racing on the Wisconsin River, and balloon racing, featuring hot air balloons, to the antics of make-believe characters, and live shows four times daily at Storybook Gardens, a 10-acre fairyland. There are helicopter rides, a professional theatre June through August, sea plane tours, a railway museum, the Tommy Bartlett Water Show, trapeze artists, and more.

Take route 23 out of the Wisconsin Dells crowds to Mirror Lake State Park, and then head east to the Wisconsin River and the town of Portage, where you can visit Fort Winnebago. Follow the bikeway along the river to Merrimac, where there is a free ferry across the river. The Merrimac area borders Lake Wisconsin, a lake formed of the Wisconsin River when the power and light dam at Prairie du Sac was constructed. Head back northwest to Devil's Lake, an eight mile bike away.

There's nothing
like the feeling
of coasting down
a long hill
on a sunny day.

LOCATION:
40 miles west of Madison in southern Wisconsin. Sauk and
   Columbia counties.

TERRAIN:
Gently rolling.

TRAVEL:
About 90 miles.

TIME:
2–3 days.

ROAD SURFACE:
Paved.

TYPE OF TRIP:
Tour or camp.

WHEN TO GO:
Spring through fall.

ROUTE:
Begin at Devil's Lake State Park. North on A to 12/23, north on 23 to Wisconsin Dells, east past Lake Delton and Mirror Lake State Park to Wisconsin Bikeway, east to U (Ice Age Bikeway), east to jog, north under I-90/94 where U turns south. In Columbia County take the Ice Age Bikeway along the Wisconsin River east to Portage to 33, south to U, south to Merrimac to 113 to Wisconsin Bikeway northwest to Devil's Lake State Park.

CAMPING:
Rocky Arbor State Park, Baraboo. 89 sites. Showers, picnicking, rocky ledges, wooded hills. North of Wisconsin Dells. 608/254-2333.

Mirror Lake State Park. Showers, picnicking, swimming, canoeing. 608/254-2333.

Devil's Lake State Park. 471 sites. Showers, concessions, nature center, hiking, picnicking, swimming, canoeing, bluff and mountain scenery. 608/356-8301.

INFORMATION:
Baraboo Chamber of Commerce, 520 Ash Street, 53913. 608/356-8333.

Wisconsin Dells Chamber of Commerce, 115 Wisconsin Avenue, P.O. Box 175, 53956. 608/254-8088.

Merrimac Chamber of Commerce, P.O. Box 64, 53561. 608/493-2340.

Baraboo and the Wisconsin Dells Trip Map

LODGING:

The Barn Motel, Baraboo. Three miles south on State 123.
Restaurant. 608/356-5511.

Spinning Wheel Motel, 809 Eighth Street, Baraboo. Reservation deposit required during season. 608/356-3933.

Birchcliff Lodge. Two miles north off River Road, Wisconsin
Dells. Heated pool. May–October 1. 608/254-7515.

Coachlight Motel, 827 Cedar Street, Wisconsin Dells. May
1–November 1. Deposit with reservations. 608/254-7917.

Lakeside Motel and Cottages. Three miles south on U.S. 12
and state 23. On Lake Delton. Restaurant, heated pool.
Outside of Wisconsin Dells. 608/253-2282.

RESTAURANTS:

Farm Kitchen. On route F at entrance to Devil's Lake State
Park.

Call of the Wild. On west edge of Wisconsin Dells.

Henny Penny Kitchen Inne Restaurant. On U.S. 12 and Lake
Avenue. Wisconsin Dells.

BIKE CARE:

Baraboo Sporting Goods, 111 Second Street, Baraboo.
608/356-6022.

Roy's Bike Shop, Highway 12 and Carpenter Street, Baraboo.
608/356-3796.

TRANSPORTATION:

Train between Wisconsin Dells and Portage. Bus between
Wisconsin Dells and Portage. Air service to Madison.

MISSISSIPPI RIVER FROM LACROSSE TO CASSVILLE TRIP*

This is river country, with bluffs, valleys, and bottom lands
scoured out by the Mississippi River that challenge your
stamina and delight your senses. Camp at LaCrosse, where

---

*Route courtesy of Joseph E. Bares, Belgium, Wisconsin.

you start your trip south along the east bank of the Mississippi River. The G. Heileman Brewing Company in town has free weekday tours at 925 South Third Street, if you are interested, or visit the Myrick Park Zoo.

As this is a linear trip, use one of three methods to get back to your car. Make a 120-mile car shuttle between Potosi and LaCrosse (hardly worth it for a two to three day trip), bus, or thumb, your way back, or get enough bikers to make two independent groups of from two to six persons each. One group starts on either end of the trip, meets in the middle to exchange car locations and keys, and drives the other group's car to a predetermined meeting place. (See Chapter 4.) By using the last method, you eliminate the need to retrace your path.

The 60 miles from LaCrosse to Prairie du Chien is moderate pedaling along the Mississippi River, but in the summer months, the road is busy with recreational vehicles and cars. If you can, make this a mid-week trip. Take a few extra days, too, to attend a festival in LaCrosse, or see some of the fascinating historical sights between Prairie du Chien and Cassville.

The steep topography south of Prairie du Chien is a challenge to even the seasoned biker, so give yourself time for plenty of rest stops where you can catch your breath and enjoy the view. The scenery here is unique; at times you ride along the river with bluffs on your left and across the river. Wildfowl abound, and you may see a blue heron strutting along the banks or soaring overhead.

Ten miles south of LaCrosse is the town of Stoddard, which lies partly on the lowland, partly on the face of a gentle, sloping bluff. Like many river villages, this one sprouted around the shacks of fishermen and woodcutters.

Genoa, settled by Italian fishermen and farmers, is a town where the now extinct passenger pigeon was once so plentiful that, as millions of them flew overhead, the townspeople were able to stand on the bluffs behind the village and knock them out of the air with long willow branches. One year, nesting pigeons covered the islands in the river for seven miles up and downstream from Genoa. The passenger pigeon became an Eastern delicacy and its feathers were popular trim for hats and decorations, which hastened its demise.

A marker in the Blackhawk Memorial Park points out the probable site of the battle of Bad Axe, fought on August 1-2, 1832, against the Indian chief, Black Hawk. This skirmish ended the Black Hawk War, and led indirectly to the settlement of Wisconsin.

In the next 34 miles from Genoa, you pass several faded villages resting on the river bluffs. The town of Desoto has an interesting wood carving museum, and the Cheese Factory in Ferryville has an observation area where you can watch cheese being made.

At Prairie du Chien, the second oldest settlement in the state, the Mississippi River flows languidly around innumerable islands. Here Joliet and Marquette first viewed the confluence of the Mississippi and Wisconsin rivers, and it soon became an important gathering place, as Indians, with colorfully painted bodies, came with great packs of fur to swap with traders and voyageurs strutting about in bright scarves, buckskin, earrings, and bracelets.

French people who settled here before 1761 named the town after a Fox Indian Chief whom they called "Le Chien," French for "dog."

The Villa Louis Mansion, built and then filled with art and literary treasures by Hercules Louis Dousman, a fur trader, has been refurnished to appear as elegant as it was a century ago. The "Prairie Gal," a replica of an old paddlewheel steamer, offers river cruises from the mansion.

The Museum of Medical Progress in town features a rare collection of space hardware, moon rocks, and mementos of the Wisconsin men involved in space flights.

Stay overnight in Prairie du Chien and rest well, for the next morning you have a steep climb of almost a mile.

Stop at Wyalusing State Park and see Sentinel Ridge, which has densely wooded parks, canyons, valleys, caves, and waterfalls. Admission. Lookout Point towers over the two rivers.

Some grades on the road to Cassville are as long as two

miles; after muscling or walking your bike up them, be sure the brake pads are securely in place before beginning the ride down.

At Cassville, a restored rural village of the 1890s called Stonefield was recreated by the State Historical Society and is open to the public. Ride into another era as a horsedrawn omnibus carries you across a covered bridge to the village square hitching rails. Watch a blacksmith at work, a printer publishing the Stonefield Gazette, or listen to hymns accompanied by a foot-powered organ.

The Nelson Dewey Farmstead State Park was originally a plantation of Wisconsin's first governor. The Dewey home and other gothic stone buildings, and the State Farm Museum, which tells the story of Wisconsin agriculture, are open to the public.

In fall, you may catch a glimpse of eagles and hawks that winter in the wooded cliffs of the Mississippi River near Cassville. They are attracted by the steady supply of food found in the screen of the Nelson Dewey Generating Station at Cassville, which discharges fish and other debris back into the Mississippi River.

Four miles down from Cassville is Potosi, the end of your trip. The town's main industry is the Potosi Brewing Company, in operation since 1852. The site was chosen because of the pure, fresh spring water which flows in the area.

LOCATION:
Southwestern Wisconsin along the Mississippi River in La-
Crosse, Vernon, Crawford, and Grant counties.

TERRAIN:
Hilly.

TRAVEL:
About 120 miles.

TIME:
2-3 days.

ROAD SURFACE:
Paved.

TYPE OF TRIP:
Tour or camp.

ROUTE:
Begin in LaCrosse. Take 35 south to Prairie du Chien, an easy
55 miles. (If you are meeting another biking group from
Potosi, wait in the small restaurant at the Jct of 35 and 27
on the northwest corner.) Camp or lodge in Prairie du
Chien and visit local attractions. Begin early for the
rigorous part of this trip. Take 35 south to Bridgeport,
across Wisconsin River to C, west three miles to X,
south two miles to P (into Bagley) to A, southeast to 133
to Cassville and Potosi.

WHEN TO GO:
Summer through fall.
In fall, LaCrosse holds a week-long Oktoberfest with street
dancing, beer drinking, and brat eating. In spring the
city, which is the square dancing capital of the world,
holds its annual "Spring Fling."

CAMPING:
Big River Campsites. Prairie du Chien. On the Mississippi
River. 93 sites. Shower, laundry, boating. One mile west
of Highway 18/35/60. South edge of Prairie du Chien.
608/326/2717.
Lake View Resorts. Three miles north of Prairie du Chien, at
Glenmore Lake.
Wyalusing State Park outside of Bagley. 131 sites. Showers,
concessions. 608/996-2261.
Goose Island Park. Ten miles south of LaCrosse on 35.
608/784-4888.
Veteran's Memorial Park. Ten miles east of LaCrosse on
Highway 16, on Trout Pond.
Grant River Public Use Area. Town Road. One mile south of
Potosi on the Mississippi River.

Mississippi River from LaCrosse to Cassville Trip Map

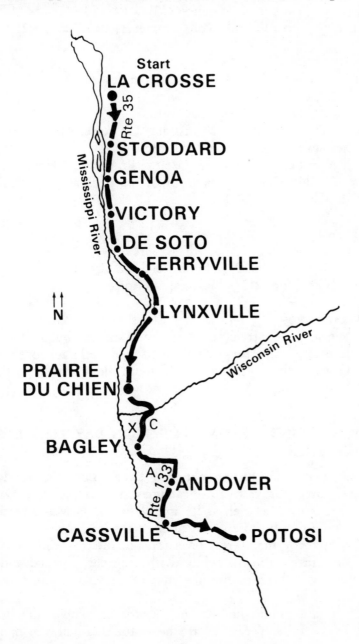

INFORMATION:
LaCrosse Chamber of Commerce, Box 842, 54601.
Prairie du Chien Chamber of Commerce, Box 326, 53821.

RESTAURANTS:
Hoffman House in LaCrosse. Two miles south on U.S. 53 south of I-90.
Mai Tai, 1539 Rose Street, LaCrosse.
Walt's, Third Street and Mississippi, LaCrosse. The bar in this restaurant is said to be LaCrosse's oldest.
Black Angus on Highway 18/35/60 in Prairie du Chien.
Beisler's Blue Heaven Supper Club, 102 S. Beaumont, Prairie du Chien.

BIKE CARE:
Smith Bicycle Shop, 520 S. 9th, La Crosse.
Gene's Bicycle Shop, 2242 State Road, La Crosse.
Glen's Bike Shop, 2137 Onalaska, LaCrosse.

TRANSPORTATION:
Air service and train to LaCrosse and Dubuque, Iowa. Intercity rail from Minneapolis and Milwaukee to La-Crosse. Bus to LaCrosse and south along the Mississippi River to DeSoto.

DOOR COUNTY FROM STURGEON BAY TO GILLS ROCK TRIP

This peninsula, jutting out into Lake Michigan, has long been known for festivals, Scandinavian food, cherry wine, cheese factories, as well as its annual Peninsula Music Festival each August, and professional summer stock theatre.

Bikers favor the scenic, level terrain. In springtime, cherry blossoms turn orchards white with fragrant flowers, and in autumn crisp breezes fire the maples and oaks with vibrant colors.

Even in summer, despite the crowds of people, the inlets and bays of the peninsula are beautiful, the sun warm, and

Overlook tower
in one of
Door County's
picturesque
state parks.

breezes refreshing. The bike route here is flat, but it can be windy.

Sturgeon Bay, where you begin your tour, is the ship building capital of the Great Lakes. Many yachts are built here and the waters around the 205 mile peninsula shoreline are dotted with sailboats.

Door County Museum is located at Fourth and Michigan avenues in the city, and has replicas of 19th century sailing ships, a genuine "chicken plucker," which is used to clean off feathers from chickens, a hand-operated fog horn, and other unusual exhibits. Nearly all of the artifacts are donated by Door County residents. The museum is open May 15 through October 15.

At Cave Point on the east coast of the peninsula, near Clark

Lake, the trail is gravel surface, but the view of lakes on either side of you is worth the inconvenience.

Further north, The Ridges Sanctuary at Bailey's Harbor is a National Natural Landmark. Once a pioneer home, the building is now a nature center with nature trails.

A 40-minute ferry ride goes from the tip of the peninsula at Gills Rock to Washington Island, which has 100 miles of roads and overnight lodging. It is one of the few places in the U.S. where both orchids and evergreens grow. Some orchids are no bigger than your thumb.

The ferry operates every hour during the peak months of July, August, and September and somewhat less frequently in the spring and fall. You can also take a ferry from either Gills Rock or Washington Island to Rock Island. The Rock Island Ferry leaves less frequently than the Washington Island Ferry from Gills Rock. Check departure and arrival times of the ferry if you plan to camp on Rock Island, so that you can schedule them into your trip. Rock Island is a lovely wooded place with no roads but with overnight camping facilities at Rock Island State Beach Park. Staying overnight on the island before starting back down the Door County peninsula is a treat.

The lighthouse at the Porte Des Morts Strait is on the National Register of Historical Places, and excavations show that the area was occupied by several cultures in prehistoric times.

Visit the marine museums at Cana Island, Gills Rock, and in Sturgeon Bay. The west side of the peninsula celebrates "Old Ellison Bay Days" on the last Saturday in June with parades, canoe jousting, relay races, and family picnics.

Fish Creek holds an Annual Fish Creek Peninsula Day, with Venetian Night boat parades, art fairs, special musical events, corn-and-brat cookouts, bake sales, and other festivities. You can also see students of the Hang Gliding Flight School in action at Fish Creek, watch the Peninsula Players perform in the Theatre-In-A-Garden, or listen to the many fine music festivals.

When biking the Door County peninsula, keep off highways 42 and 57 as much as possible, as there can be heavy truck traffic on these roads. The county roads along the shoreline are much more quiet and scenic, and virtually all of them are paved.

LOCATION:
Northeastern Wisconsin on Door County peninsula.

TERRAIN:
Flat.

TRAVEL:
100 miles round trip.

TIME:
2 days (plus 2 or more days on Washington and Rock islands).

ROAD SURFACE:
Mostly paved. Some gravel travel on the east coast.

TYPE OF TRIP:
Day, tour, or camp.

ROUTE:
Begin at Sturgeon Bay. Take County B north to G, north to 42 (through Peninsula State Park) to Gills Rock. Ferry to Washington Island and bike on island. Ferry to Rock Island for camping. Return by ferry to mainland. Retrace 42 south to 57, south to Q, east and south to 57, south (to Jacksonport) to Clark Lake Road, south to T, south and west to Sturgeon Bay.

WHEN TO GO:
Spring through fall (crowded on weekends; try for mid-week tours).

CAMPING:

Peninsula State Park at Fish Creek. 457 sites. Showers, food. 414/868-3258.

Potowatomi State Park at Sturgeon Bay. 125 sites. 414/743-5123.

Rock Island State Park on Rock Island. 40 sites. Ferry. 414/847-2235.

Newport State Park, Ellison Bay. Hiking trails. 13 backpack sites. 414/854-2500.

INFORMATION:

Door County Chamber of Commerce, Green Bay Road, Sturgeon Bay, 54235.

LODGING:

Cliff Dwellers Motel. Sturgeon Bay. 1¼ mile south on 42/57. 2 miles north on Duluth Avenue. 414/743-4260. April-Labor Day.

Holiday. 29 N. Second Avenue. 414/743-5571. Sturgeon Bay.

Harbor Lights Motel on 42 in town. Egg Harbor.

Shallows. Egg Harbor. 2 miles south on G off 42. 414/868-3458.

By-the-Bay. Fish Creek. Box 253. 414/868-3456.

Stewart's Peninsula. Fish Creek. Box 246. ½ mile north on 42. 414/868-3281.

On Washington Island: Viking Village. 2 miles northeast of ferry dock. 414/847-2551.

On Washington Island: Wright's Holiday Inn. 2½ miles northeast of ferry dock. Volleyball. 414/847-2526.

Parent Motel. Bailey's Harbor. 1 mile north on 57. 414/839-2218.

Sands. Bailey's Harbor. Box 114. Volleyball. 414/839-2401.

RESTAURANTS:

Leathem Smith Lodge. Sturgeon Bay. 414/743-5555.

Tony's Fiesta. Fish Creek. ½ mile north on 42, near Peninsula State Park entrance. 414/868-3316.

Door County from Sturgeon Bay to Gills Rock Map

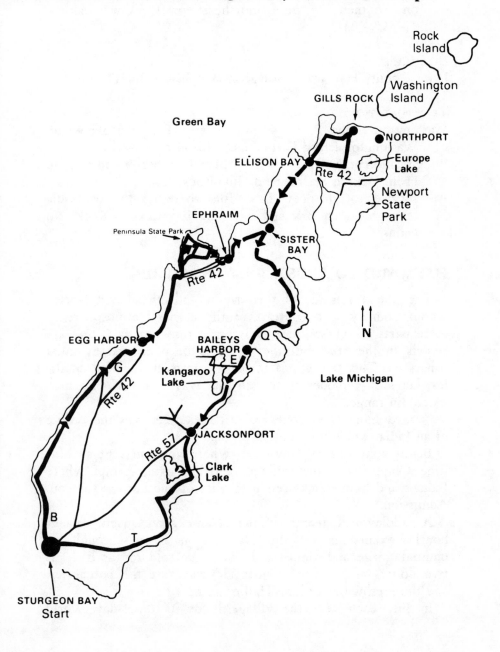

Rock Island

Washington Island

GILLS ROCK

Green Bay

NORTHPORT

ELLISON BAY

Rte 42

Europe Lake

Newport State Park

EPHRAIM

Peninsula State Park

SISTER BAY

Rte 42

N

EGG HARBOR

BAILEYS HARBOR

Q

G

E

Rte 42

Kangaroo Lake

Lake Michigan

Rte 57

JACKSONPORT

Clark Lake

B

T

STURGEON BAY
Start

Gordon Lodge. Bailey's Harbor on North Bay ½ mile north on 57 then 6½ miles northeast on Q. Own baking. 414/839-2331.

BIKE CARE:
Door County Hardware. Sturgeon Bay. 414/743-4417.

TRANSPORTATION:
Washington Island Ferry. 40-minute trip. For schedule write: Washington Island Ferry Line, Ellison Bay, 54210.
Rock Island Ferry. Operates from June–October, 9 a.m.–4 p.m. From Jackson Harbor and Gills Rock.
Air service to Sturgeon Bay. Bus route up the peninsula through Green Bay and Sturgeon Bay to Gills Rock. No trains.

HAYWARD TO APOSTLE ISLANDS TRIP

The placid solitude of this trip in Indianhead and Northwoods country is a contrast to the carnival atmosphere of some parts of the southern Wisconsin resort areas. There are resorts in the area, but they tend to be populated by quiet fishermen. This trip winds through forests and around countless lakes on a moderate terrain that was once part of a high mountain range.

Named Indianhead country, this area resembles the profile of an Indian when you look at a map.

Begin your trip in Hayward, where you can visit an old-time Chippewa Indian village, and a logging camp, where Indians and lumberjacks relive the life of another era for you. Admission.

A paddlewheel steamboat, the "Namekagon Queen," makes hourly excursions on the Namekagon River through an unusual gorge and along land that once sold for as little as two dollars an acre. Also near Hayward are fish hatcheries, and the Freshwater Fishing Hall of Fame.

In July each year the village holds its three-day World

Lumberjack Championships, where you can watch contests in wood chopping, log rolling, and other activities.

You pass three Indian reservations and 30 miles of shoreline along Lake Gitchee Gumee, the Indian name for Lake Superior.

The climax of your trip is at Bayfield, a tiny waterfront town with the flavor of a New England fishing village. Fishing has always been the mainstay of this 125-year-old village.

Abundant water and warm weather in this area make biting insects common from May to mid-September. Insect repellents provide some relief but the best protection is to wear clothing that covers your arms, neck, and legs when you are off your bike, particularly in the evening and morning. A splendid assortment of wildflowers carpets the ground in this area from May to October. Indian paintbrush, violets, goldenrods, thistles, asters, and even orchids are just a few of the flowers that add their color to the seasons.

By taking an extra week, you can extend your trip and take the 15-minute ferry from Bayfield to La Pointe on Madeline Island, the largest of the 22 Apostle Islands, just off the tip of the northern Wisconsin mainland. Madeline Island has a rich history from 4,000 B.C., when Indians used the island.

More recent history dates back to the time of Columbus, when the rugged isle was a Chippewa stronghold. It was a stopping place for the French voyageurs, and later became a fur trading, fishing and logging center.

Most of the island roads are sand or gravel, so bring a heavy duty 10-speed bike, or plan to hike. Seven miles from La Pointe, Big Bay State Park has campsites where you can enjoy the special serenity that only island living offers. A concession at Little Sand Bay provides fuel, groceries, and camping and fishing supplies.

LOCATION:

Northwestern Wisconsin in Sawyer, Ashland, and Douglas counties.

TERRAIN:
Moderately hilly.

TRAVEL:
About 200 miles (more if you stay on Madeline Island).

TIME:
5 days plus time on Madeline Island.

ROAD SURFACE:
Paved, except for several gravel and sand roads on Madeline
    Island.

TYPE OF TRIP:
Tour or camp.

ROUTE:
Begin in Hayward. Take 77 east (to Mellen) to 13, northwest
    (to Ashland) to 13, north to Bayfield. Ferry to Madeline
    Island. Return. Take 13 west along shoreline of Lake
    Superior and then south to H, south (to Brule) to 27,
    south to 77, east and south to Hayward.

WHEN TO GO:
Spring through fall. Bring warm clothing and insect repellent
    at any time of year.

CAMPING:
Day Lake Campground (National Forest). One mile north of
    Clam Lake on GG. 25 sites. Lake swimming.
Copper Falls State Park. Mellen. 4 miles northeast via 13. 34
    sites. Nature hikes. Lake swimming.
Northwoods Motel Trailer Park. 36 sites. Hot showers,
    laundry. Ashland. From east city limits, 1½ mile east on
    U.S. 2.
Prentice Park. Ashland. In town on 2 and 13. 40 sites.

Memorial Park. Washburn. North of town off 13. 50 sites. Hot showers, phone, lake swimming.

Apostle Island View Campground. Bayfield. From south city limits ½ mile on 13 then 14 miles west on J, then ¼ mile north on Court Road. 39 sites. Showers, grocery.

Dalrymple City Park. Bayfield. North of town on 13. 20 sites.

Little Sand Bay City Park. Bayfield. 5 miles north on 13, 5 miles north on K, 3 miles north on Sand Bay Road. 11 sites.

Harbor View Campground. Cornucopia. From center of town ¼ mile east on 13. 38 sites.

Brule Campground. Brule. At west city limits on 2. 21 sites. Showers. April–December 1.

INFORMATION:

Hayward Chamber of Commerce, 125 West 1st Street, Box 283. 715/634-4801.

Sawyer County Recreation Association, Box 486W, Hayward, 54834.

Ashland Area Chamber of Commerce, 111 Front St. West. 54806.

Bayfield County Recreation, Washburn, 54891.

LODGING:

Rocky Run Resort. Washburn. Spring through fall. 715/373-2551.

Holiday House Motel. 46 rooms. Restaurant. Ashland. 715/682-5235.

Ashland Motel. Ashland. 22 rooms. 715/682-5503.

RESTAURANTS:

Logging Camp Cook Shanty. Hayward. In city.

Tony's Fireside. Northwoods Beach area in Hayward.

Ranch Supper Club on 77 one mile east of Hayward.

Scottie Club. Ashland. 14 miles west on 13. Reservations.

Golden Glow Restaurant. Ashland. 519 West Second Street.

Hayward to Apostle Islands Trip Map

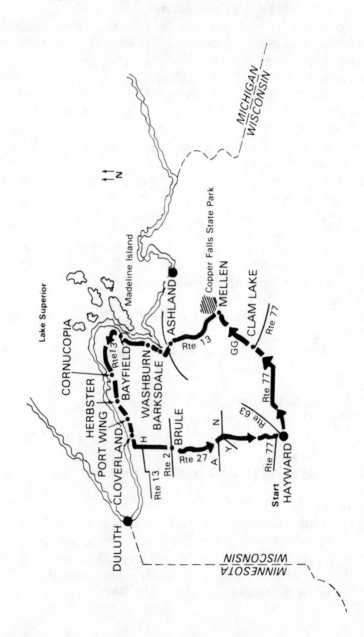

BIKE CARE:

Bodin's Seaway Marina and Bike Repair. Ashland. 715/682-6441.

Boudreaus' Bike Shop. Ashland. 715/682-9132.

TRANSPORTATION:

Air service to Ashland and Hayward. Bus through Hayward and Ashland. Train to Duluth, Minnesota, west of Bayfield.

11

How to Plan Your Own Route

If you have a road, you have a bike trip. With this remark, some would-be bikers dismiss the whole notion of planning a tour. You can bike down many roads in this country, but not all of them are smooth and scenic, and very few of them combine plenty of restaurants, campsites, and rest stops with little or no traffic.

To make finding a quiet forest and cool water at the end of your biking day more than chance, and to take precautions against biking on a brick road—yellow *or* red, which wears out bike and body quickly—plan your trip.

The trails in this book are designed to get you into some of the lovely areas in the Midwest, but there are many other lovely areas that cry out to be seen and enjoyed. Expand on the trips in this book, or make entirely new trails in other parts of the state. If you like, you can even plan bike tours of other countries.

Two factors to consider when making a route you can

Plan your own route around some scenic place you've always wanted to visit.

handle with pleasure are the riding experience of those in your group, and their interests. Find an area that everyone will enjoy, and plan a route that is neither too hard, nor too easy for them.

Bike a shorter distance than you think everyone can handle; this will assure a nice trip, and allow for unexpected delights such as a nap in a sunny park, a stop at a charming restaurant, or a spur-of-the-moment hike to a panoramic overlook.

Carry an emergency snack and water on a one-day trip, and bring money to get you home in case you have major bike trouble. Or have a phone number where you can reach someone who will come and pick you up if you need a ride.

If you take a weekend tour of the country, bring almost all of the food you will need. In small towns most businesses, stores, and restaurants are closed on Sunday, so don't count on eating out or buying food then, unless you are in a resort town. The most you may get is juice or milk at a local gas station.

Your first consideration in planning a trip is, where will you go? This will be determined, in part, by your interests. Do you like architecture? Take a trip through Chicago and its suburbs, and see classic examples of Frank Lloyd Wright, Louis Sullivan and other, contemporary styles of architecture.

If archeology is your avocation, bike to one of the many areas where Indian mounds are being excavated.

It's possible to combine fishing and biking as long as you only bring back *tales* of the big one that got away. Anything you actually catch should be eaten immediately. The motto for eating fish after you catch it is, "the sooner the better." You don't want to carry a limp fish around on your bike.

Combine biking with swimming, hiking, canoeing, and many other outdoor activities. Bike to circuses, county fairs, and museums. Or combine history, nature study and exercise on a trip with young children. Choose a destination where you learn about nuclear power stations, or ride to a chemistry convention. All of these are compatible with biking.

Perhaps you want to escape into the wilderness. Bike there. If you're willing to sacrifice the smoothness of paved roads, and have a sturdy, heavy-weight bike, you can get into areas of utterly deserted back country by taking dirt and gravel roads.

Whatever your interests, biking towards them makes them more enjoyable.

How do you decide where to go? Something as complicated as researching an area in your library, or as simple as looking through a picture book, may spark your interest. Your child may have studied a particular geographical area in school, or maybe you studied about an area as a child, and it has intrigued you ever since. A friend may recommend a place, or your senses may simply yearn for a different landscape— mountains, perhaps, or prairie, or ocean front.

What are your limitations? Time, money, experience, and equipment. These are a few considerations to take into account. If you have only a weekend, bike someplace within 200 miles of home. Drive that distance within four hours, and then bike in the area.

If you have little money, camp out. If you have little experience, take short trips at first, and keep within hiking distance of a phone or gas station. If you have no lightweight equipment, you can have a lot of fun taking day trips in various areas.

What can you see in an area? Stop at your library and look in books and pamphlets. The American Guide Service has books on each state, originally written as a Federal Writer's Project during the Depression, which describe the topography, archeology, history, politics, culture and cities and towns, and give several sight-seeing tours. Parallel a bike trip along one of these auto tours, taking back roads instead of major highways.

Oil company travel guides, and auto club tour guides give useful information such as points of interest, lodging and restaurants in different areas. These books are available in many libraries. The travel guides can be purchased at bookstores.

After you pick an area, write to the chambers of commerce in nearby towns for places to camp, lodge, and eat, as well as for information on local festivals and attractions. They are happy to send any information they have. Also ask if there are long stretches on your planned trip where there is no food, water, or other amenities. Ask if there is danger from any wild animals or poisonous snakes.

Local chamber of commerce addresses and zip codes are listed in the *World Wide Chamber of Commerce Directory* (published annually in July), Johnson Publishing Company, Inc., P.O. Box 455, Eighth and Van Buren, Loveland, Colorado 80537. Many libraries carry this as a reference book.

For information on motels, restaurants and local color, check *Fodor's USA,* a series of travel books written by Eugene Fodor.

One of the most thorough camping guides in print is *Woodall's Campground Directory, North American Edition,* published

Allow plenty of time for sightseeing and relaxing—though you don't necessarily have to bring a hammock.

by Woodall Publishing Company, 500 Hyacinth Place, Highland Park, Illinois 60035. This volume, which is the size of a metropolitan telephone book, and weighs several pounds, gives campgrounds, their facilities, and directions on how to get to them from the nearest highway, for all the states in the U.S.

Call the park you plan to stay at, and find out what their policies are on reservations. Most private campgrounds will accept reservations. Some state parks will, if you plan to stay 15 days or longer; others accept no reservations; a few take reservations for large parties.

Find out where the bicycle repair shops are in the area you plan to see. Often college and university libraries have telephone books of many cities. Otherwise, call the long distance operator, and get the name and phone number of a bike shop in the area. Call the shop and see what kind of service they provide.

Traveling to your take-off point is most convenient by car.

But you can take your bike on buses, trains, and planes. Here again, call in advance to find out what the regulations are regarding transporting bikes.

Another method of biking is to use hostels. The American Youth Hostels, Inc., established in 1934, maintains low cost accommodations for its members throughout the U.S. If you travel under your own power—hiking, biking, canoeing, etc.—you can use these accommodations for a small fee by becoming a member of the AYH.

The *Bicycle Atlas* of the AYH gives information on biking, plus 60 possible trips in the U.S. and abroad. Write to:

> American Youth Hostels
> National Headquarters
> 1554 First Avenue
> New York, New York 10028

If you prefer to bike with a club or organization, join the League of American Wheelmen, which has chapters all over the states. For the $8 annual membership fee you receive a free subscription to their excellent monthly magazine, *LAW Bulletin,* and are eligible to participate in any of their bike trips. Your membership dues also go for legal support and promotion of biking throughout the country. For information write:

> LAW Headquarters
> 19 South Bothwell
> Palatine, Illinois 60067
> Phone: 312/991-1200

You can also get information regarding biking trails from:

> Bicycle Institute of America
> 122 East 42nd Street
> New York, New York 10017

Boom in Bikeways gives good coverage of bike legislation, and biking facilities and programs. Available free by writing:

Bicycle Manufacturers Association of America
1101 15th Street, N. W.
Washington, D. C. 20005

If you choose to bike on your own, one of the most important things to do is map your route. Stay away from major highways featured on service station maps and stick to lightly traveled roads that wind through the country. Try to find roads that are paved, have light traffic, and hills that meet your skills.

Look at a topographical map in an atlas to get a general idea of the terrain. These maps describe the elevation of a given area through the use of contour lines. You can purchase individual topographical maps from the following government offices.

Maps east of the Mississippi:

Distribution Section
U. S. Geological Survey
1200 South Eads Street
Arlington, Virginia 22202

Maps west of the Mississippi:

Distribution Section
U. S. Geological Survey
Federal Center
Denver, Colorado 80225

A booklet, *Topographic Maps,* tells how to use these maps, and their symbols. It can be obtained free of charge from the same addresses.

The maps come in several sizes. One inch can represent one, two, or four miles, depending upon the scale you order. Allow two weeks for delivery. Many topographical maps are also available at bookstores, but they usually cost more than those ordered from the government.

After you've chosen your area and points of interest, look

at the *Rand McNally Atlas of the United States.* Each map in it
has red, blue, and black lines denoting different kinds of roads.
Route your trip along the blue lines which are local roads and
have the lightest traffic. These roads are paved. Green lines
are interstate highways, and red lines are principal through-
ways; both have heavy traffic.

Scenic roads are designated by a yellow overlay line. These
may be beautiful, but they are sometimes crowded with
drivers who also want to enjoy the scenery, especially on
weekends.

For alternate lightly traveled roads, purchase county maps
of your area for a small fee by writing to state agencies.

County maps of Illinois, Michigan, Wisconsin and Indiana
are compiled in state atlases published by the Rockford Map
Publishers, 4525 Forest View Avenue, Box 6126, Rockford,
Illinois. Your library may have a copy of each of these atlases.

Read the legends on county maps and choose roads that are
paved, whenever possible. A few miles of gravel travel can be
endured; much more is both bike and nerve wracking.

If your trip passes through a large city, stay off the roads
during rush hour traffic, and keep off main and busy arteries
as much as possible.

PERSONAL CONSIDERATIONS

After you decide where you want to go, consider the
personal factors in your bike trip. Our bodies are a marvelous
combination of about $10 worth of chemicals that, when
pedaling a bike, become the most efficient means of travel in
the world. Don't abuse them.

Plan to ride between 20 and 50 miles a day on level ground,
which is an average distance for an intermediate biker. This
should give you enough time for leisurely stops at your chosen
points of interest. If the terrain is hilly, 50 miles will be a
good workout, so take extra time. Do less, if you have young
children or older bikers with you, or if you want to relax
near a log cabin, natural spring, or waterfall. Don't by-pass
something you are interested in.

Wind is as important a factor to consider when biking as terrain. A 10-mile-an-hour headwind can exhaust hearty bikers in a short time.

On hilly terrain you have a wind-chill factor going downhill even on calm days. Put on a windbreaker for the downhill run if it's at all cool. You'll hate to interrupt that long slide down once you've started, and if you're on the shady side of the bluff, the evaporation of perspiration, plus cool air, can cause stiff muscles and chills later.

If you bike with children who are moving under their own power, make your first several trips day trips. Leave in the morning, bike for four hours and then return. For children under 12, use bike paths until they become accustomed to using hand signals and staying alert. Then try them on the highway, but keep a close watch on them in traffic.

Day trips give you a feel for the stamina of your bikers as well as an idea of what you want to take in the way of food and tools.

The next step, if you bike with children, is to settle on one campsite for a weekend and ride out from it in different directions each day.

Camp or tour for trips of more than a weekend. Camping gets you closest to nature, the people, and the area you visit. But motels are priceless on that cold, rainy night when all your equipment and clothing is drenched. Have money for them.

WEATHER

Biking enthusiasts believe there is no such thing as bad weather—only different kinds of good weather. Spring through fall are choice biking times, with summers in the Midwest being generally hot and sunny. Spring tends to be the wettest of the three seasons, not because it rains more, but because the rain comes in light and frequent showers at this time of year. In autumn, the same amount of precipitation falls, but in heavy thunderstorms spaced further apart. The clear, crisp fall weather is invigorating, but in upper Michigan, Minnesota and Wisconsin, freezing temperatures at night are not uncommon.

For pamphlets on the climate of each state write to:

> Superintendent of Documents
> U.S. Government Printing Office
> Washington, D.C. 20402

The following charts give some perspective on the temperature, rainfall, and wind in the Midwest at various times of the year, as well as the average dates for the first and last freeze in this area.

Average Date of First and Last Freeze

	Average Date of First Freeze	*Average Date of Last Freeze*
Springfield, Ill.	October 30	April 8
Detroit, Mich.	October 21	April 23
Indianapolis, Ind.	October 23	April 23
Chicago, Ill.	October 27	April 22
Flint, Mich.	October 9	May 8
Grand Rapids, Mich.	October 27	April 25
Milwaukee, Wisc.	October 19	April 25
Madison, Wisc.	Mid-October	Late April
Minneapolis, Minn	October 13	April 30
Duluth, Minn.	October 3	May 13
Des Moines, Iowa	October 19	April 20

All chart information from *Traveling Weatherwise in the USA* by Edward Powers and James Witt, Dodd Mead and Company, 1972.

Temperature Averages (in degrees Fahrenheit)

Month	Springfield, Ill.	Indianapolis, Ind.	Chicago, Ill.	Detroit, Mich.	Flint, Mich.
March	50–30	50–30	44–29	42–27	41–24
April	65–42	62–40	75–41	56–39	56–35
May	76–52	73–50	69–51	69–49	68–45
June	85–63	83–60	80–62	79–60	79–55
July	90–66	88–64	84–67	84–65	84–59
August	87–64	86–63	82–66	82–64	82–58
September	80–55	79–56	75–57	74–56	73–51
October	69–44	76–44	63–47	63–45	62–41
November	52–32	51–33	47–33	47–34	46–30

Temperature Averages (in degrees Fahrenheit)

Month	Grand Rapids, Mich.	Milwaukee, Wisc.	Madison, Wisc.	Minneapolis, Minn.	Duluth, Minn.	Des Moines, Iowa
March	42–24	41–26	42–23	39–23	31–13	43–25
April	57–35	53–36	57–35	56–36	46–28	59–38
May	69–45	64–45	69–46	69–48	60–39	71–50
June	79–56	75–55	79–56	79–58	70–49	81–61
July	85–60	81–61	86–60	85–63	77–56	87–65
August	83–58	79–61	83–58	82–61	75–55	85–63
September	74–50	72–53	74–51	73–52	65–46	77–54
October	73– 0	60–42	61–40	60–41	53–35	66–43
November	46–28	45–30	44–27	41–25	34–20	47–28

Average Monthly Precipitation (in inches)

Month	Springfield, Ill.	Indianapolis, Ind.	Chicaro, Ill.	Detroit, Mich.	Flint, Mich.
March	3	4	3	2	2
April	4	4	3	3	3
May	4	4	4	4	3
June	4	4	4	3	3
July	3	3	3	3	3
August	3	4	3	3	3
September	3	4	3	2	3
October	3	3	3	3	2
November	2	3	2	2	2

Average Monthly Precipitation (in inches)

Month	Grand Rapids, Mich.	Milwaukee, Wisc.	Madison, Wisc.	Minneapolis, Minn.	Duluth, Minn.	Des Moines, Iowa
March	2	2	2	1	2	1
April	3	2	2	2	3	2
May	3	3	3	3	3	2
June	3	3	4	4	4	3
July	3	2	3	3	4	2
August	3	3	3	3	3	3
September	3	3	4	3	3	2
October	3	2	2	2	2	1
November	2	2	2	1	2	1

Monthly Prevailing Winds
(miles per hour and direction)

Month	Springfield, Ill.	Indianapolis, Ind.	Chicago, Ill.	Detroit, Mich.	Flint, Mich.
March	14NW	14WNW	12W	12NW	13WNW
April	14S	13W	12W	11NW	12NNW
May	12SSW	11SW	10SSW	10S	11WSW
June	10SSW	9SW	9SW	9S	9SW
July	8SSW	8SW	8SW	8S	8SW
August	8SSW	8NE	8SW	8N	8SW
September	8SSW	9SW	9S	9S	9S
October	11S	10SW	10S	10S	10SW
November	13S	13W	11SSW	11SW	12SSW

Monthly Prevailing Winds
(miles per hour and direction)

Month	Grand Rapids, Mich.	Milwaukee, Wisc.	Madison, Wisc.	Minneapolis, Minn.	Duluth, Minn.	Des Moines, Iowa
March	12S	14WNW	13NW	12NW	14WNW	14NW
April	12W	14NNE	13NW	13NW	15NW	14NW
May	10W	13NNE	11WSW	12SE	14E	12SE
June	9S	11NNE	10S	11SE	12E	11S
July	8W	10SW	9S	10SE	11E	10S
August	8W	10SW	9S	9SE	11E	9S
September	9SSW	11SW	10S	10SSE	12WNW	10S
October	9SSW	12SW	10S	11SE	13WNW	11S
November	11SSW	14WNW	12W	12NW	14NW	12NW

Index